INTRODUCTION

It is my hope that this book will encourage
new quilters to make a variety of projects
using our simple and clear instructions. The quilts
chosen for this book are tried and true favorites from
the **Thimbleberries Collection**. They offer a wide
variety of choices in size, design, and technique.
Before you begin a project, it is very important to read
through **Getting Started**.   Also, take time to
read through **Tips**, and **Hints and Helps** given
throughout **Beginner's Luck**. They explain why
certain steps are important and will also help to build
your confidence and skills.   The **General Instructions**
are a reference for techniques that are repeated from
project to project. **Beginner's Luck** includes tips that
will help you achieve successful piecing accuracy, and
an overall enjoyment of the whole creative process.
Good (Beginner's) Luck . . .

My Best,
Lynette Jensen

Thank you to the Staff of Thimbleberries® Design Studio;
Sue Bahr, Lisa Kirchoff, Kathy Lobeck, Ardelle Paulson,
Sherry Husske, Virginia Brodd, Renae Ashwill,
Julie Jergens, Tracy Schrantz, Clarine Howe, Pearl Baysinger, Ellen Carter,
and quilters Julie Borg, Quilter's Heaven, and Country Loft Quilt and Design.

Published by
Publishing Solutions, LLC
2615 Christian Court
Chaska, MN 55318
952-361-4902
James L. Knapp, President
www.ipubsolutions.com

Cover Design by Laurel Albright

Production Management
Book Productions, LLC

1 2 3 4 5 6 / 07 06 05 04 03
ISBN 0-9725580-1-2

Beginner's Luck

by Lynette Jensen

CONTENTS

BIG PUMPKIN, LITTLE PUMPKIN

Yardage is based on 42-inch wide fabric.

FABRICS AND SUPPLIES

1/4	yard	**ORANGE PRINT #1** for large pumpkin
8-inch square		**ORANGE PRINT #2** for small pumpkin
8-inch square		**ORANGE PRINT #3** for small pumpkin
3/8	yard	**BEIGE PRINT** for background and checkerboard border
5/8	yard	**BROWN PRINT** for pumpkin stems and outer border
1/4	yard	**GREEN PRINT #1** for leaves
1/3	yard	**BLACK PRINT** for inner border and corner squares
1/4	yard	**GREEN PRINT #2** for checkerboard border
1/3	yard	**BLACK PRINT** for binding
1	yard	Backing fabric

Quilt batting, at least 34 x 38-inches

A rotary cutter, mat, and wide clear plastic ruler with 1/8-inch markings are needed tools in attaining accuracy. A 6 x 24-inch ruler and 12-1/2-inch acrylic square are recommended.

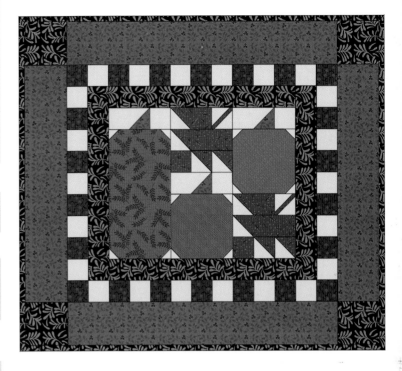

30 x 34-inches

GETTING STARTED

❖ Read instructions thoroughly before beginning project.

❖ Prewash and press fabrics to test for color fastness and possible shrinkage.

❖ For piecing, place right sides of fabric pieces together and use 1/4-inch seam allowances throughout unless otherwise specified.

❖ It is very important that accurate 1/4-inch seam allowances are used. It is wise to stitch a sample 1/4-inch seam allowance to check your machine's seam allowance accuracy.

❖ Press seam allowances in one direction toward the darker fabric and/or in the direction that will create the least bulk.

❖ Instructions are given for quick cutting and piecing of blocks. Note that for some of the pieces, the quick-cutting method will result in leftover fabric.

TIP . . . .

To make the pumpkins stand out, select 3 separate orange fabrics that have different print motifs and scale. Perhaps a plaid and a stripe fabric combined with a print would make a nice combination. The strongest fabric, either color or design, should be used in the smaller pumpkin. This will help keep the different size pumpkins visually balanced. The two green leaf blocks could be made from the two different but coordinating green fabrics.

TIP . . . .

Stitch on the outer edge just a "hair" or a thread width from the marked diagonal line.

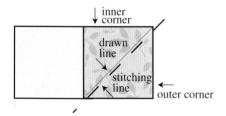

If you stitch on the inner corner side of the diagonal line you will actually make the triangle smaller.

PUMPKIN BLOCKS

Make 1 large pumpkin
Make 2 small pumpkins

Cutting

From **ORANGE PRINT #1**:
*   Cut 1, 6-1/2 x 12-1/2-inch rectangle

From **ORANGE PRINT #2**:
*   Cut 1, 6-1/2-inch square

From **ORANGE PRINT #3**:
*   Cut 1, 6-1/2-inch square

From **BEIGE PRINT**:
*   Cut 1, 2-1/2 x 42-inch strip. From this strip cut:
        3, 2-1/2 x 4-1/2-inch rectangles
        3, 2-1/2-inch squares
        12, 1-1/2-inch squares

From **BROWN PRINT**:
*   Cut 3, 2-1/2-inch squares

Piecing

Step 1

Position 1-1/2-inch **BEIGE** squares on the corners of the 6-1/2 x 12-1/2-inch **ORANGE #1** rectangle. Draw a diagonal line on each square and stitch on the lines. Trim the seam allowances to 1/4-inch and press. Repeat this process with the 6-1/2-inch **ORANGE #2** and **ORANGE #3** squares .

Make 1 large pumpkin   Make 2 small pumpkins

Step 2

Position a 2-1/2-inch **BROWN** square on the right side of a 2-1/2 x 4-1/2-inch **BEIGE** rectangle. Draw a diagonal line on the square, stitch, trim, and press toward the dark fabric. Add a 2-1/2-inch **BEIGE** square to the right side of this unit and press toward the light fabric. <u>At this point each stem unit should measure 2-1/2 x 6-1/2-inches.</u> Referring to the quilt diagram, sew the stem units to the top of the Step 1 pumpkin units and press.

Make 3

LEAF BLOCKS

Cutting

From **GREEN PRINT #1**:
- Cut 2, 2-7/8-inch squares
- Cut 1, 2-1/2 x 42-inch strip. From this strip cut:
  - 2, 2-1/2 x 6-1/2-inch rectangles
  - 2, 2-1/2 x 4-1/2-inch rectangles
  - 2, 2-1/2-inch squares
  - 2, 1 x 4-1/2-inch stem strips

From **BEIGE PRINT**:
- Cut 2, 2-7/8-inch squares
- Cut 2, 2-5/8-inch squares, cutting each square diagonally to make 4 triangles
- Cut 4, 2-1/2-inch squares

Piecing

Step 1

Position a 2-1/2-inch **BEIGE** square on the left side of a 2-1/2 x 4-1/2-inch **GREEN** rectangle. Draw a diagonal line on the square, stitch, trim, and press to make an upper leaf unit. Repeat this process with the 2-1/2 x 6-1/2-inch **GREEN** rectangle to make a center leaf unit.

Make 2 upper leaf units   Make 2 center leaf units

Step 2

With right sides together, layer the 2-7/8-inch **GREEN** and **BEIGE** squares together in pairs. Press together, but do not sew. Cut the layered squares in half diagonally to make 4 sets of triangles. Stitch 1/4-inch from the diagonal edge of each pair of triangles and press. <u>At this point each triangle-pieced square should measure 2-1/2-inches square.</u> Referring to the diagram, sew the triangle-pieced squares together in pairs, add a 2-1/2-inch **GREEN** square to the left edge of the unit, and press. <u>At this point each lower leaf unit should measure 2-1/2 x 6-1/2-inches.</u>

Make 4, 2-1/2-inch triangle-pieced squares   Make 2 lower leaf units

Diagonal Piecing

❖ Piece the border strips together with diagonal seams. They are less visible in a finished quilt than straight seams.

❖ To sew two border strips together diagonally, place them together at a 90° angle with right sides together, as shown below.

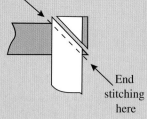

Each strip should extend approximately 1/4-inch beyond the other. Draw a diagonal line to use as your stitching guide. Sew the two strips together, taking care to start and stop your stitching precisely at the point where the two strips meet, as shown above. Trim away the excess fabric, leaving a 1/4-inch seam allowance, and press the seam open.

❖ Cut enough border strips, so after your strips are stitched together, the diagonal seams will not be at the corners of the quilt top.

Step 3

To make a leaf stem unit, center a **BEIGE** triangle on a 1 x 4-1/2-inch **GREEN** strip and stitch together with a 1/4-inch seam allowance. Center another **BEIGE** triangle on the opposite edge of the **GREEN** strip and stitch. Press the seam allowances toward the **GREEN** strip. Trim the stem unit so it measures 2-1/2-inches square. Make 2 stem units. Sew each stem unit to the right side of the Step 1 upper leaf units and press. At this point each upper leaf unit should measure 2-1/2 x 6-1/2-inches.

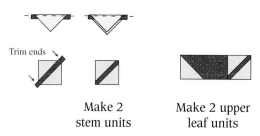

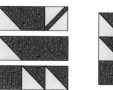

Make 2
stem units

Make 2 upper
leaf units

Step 4

Referring to the block diagram, sew the Step 1, 2, and 3 leaf units together and press. At this point each leaf block should measure 6-1/2-inches square.

Make 2

Step 5

Referring to the quilt diagram, sew together the leaf blocks and small pumpkin blocks, and press. Sew together the leaf/pumpkin sections and large pumpkin block to make the quilt center. At this point the quilt center should measure 14-1/2 x 18-1/2-inches.

BORDERS

Note: The yardage given allows for the border strips to be cut on the crosswise grain. Diagonally piece the strips as needed, referring to **Diagonal Piecing** *instructions. Read through* **Border** *instructions on page 118 for general instructions on adding borders.*

Cutting

From **BLACK PRINT**:
- Cut 4, 4-1/2-inch corner squares
- Cut 2, 2-1/2 x 42-inch inner border strips

From **GREEN PRINT #2**:
- Cut 2, 2-1/2 x 42-inch strips. From one of these strips cut: 2, 2-1/2-inch squares. The remaining strips will be used for strip sets.

From **BEIGE PRINT**:
- Cut 2, 2-1/2 x 42-inch strips. From one of these strips cut: 2, 2-1/2-inch squares. The remaining strips will be used for strip sets.

From **BROWN PRINT**:
- Cut 3, 4-1/2 x 42-inch outer border strips

Assembling and Attaching the Borders

Step 1
Attach the 2-1/2-inch wide **BLACK** inner border strips.

Step 2
Aligning long edges, sew the 2-1/2-inch wide **GREEN #2** and **BEIGE** strips together in pairs and press. Make a total of 2 strip sets. Cut the strip sets into segments.

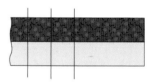

Crosscut 20, 2-1/2-inch wide segments

Step 3
To make the top and bottom checkerboard borders, sew together 5 of the Step 2 segments and press. Sew a 2-1/2-inch **BEIGE** square to one end and press. Make 2 border strips. <u>At this point each checkerboard border should measure 2-1/2 x 22-1/2-inches</u>. Sew the border strips to the quilt center and press.

Make 2 border strips

Step 4
To make the side checkerboard borders, sew together 5 of the Step 2 segments and press. Sew a 2-1/2-inch **GREEN #2** square to one end and press. Make 2 border strips. <u>At this point each checkerboard border should measure 2-1/2 x 22-1/2-inches</u>. Sew the border strips to the quilt center and press.

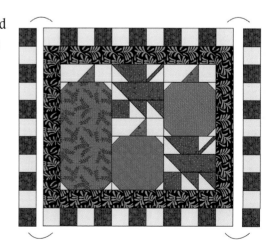

Step 5

Measure the quilt from left to right through the middle. Measure and mark the border lengths and center points on the 4-1/2 wide **BROWN** strips. Pin the border strips to the quilt, stitch, and press. Trim away the excess fabric.

Step 6

For the side borders, measure the quilt top from top to bottom including seam allowances, but not the top and bottom borders. Cut the **BROWN** side borders to this length. Sew a 4-1/2-inch **BLACK** corner square to each end of these border strips. Sew the borders to the quilt and press.

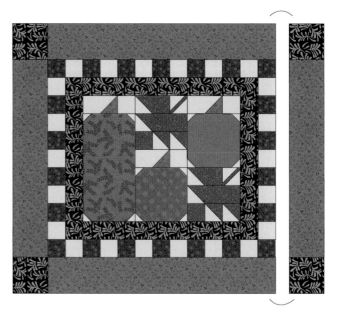

Border Assembly Diagram

PUTTING IT ALL TOGETHER

Trim the backing and batting so they are approximately 4-inches larger than the quilt top. Read through **Finishing the Quilt** on page 118 for complete instructions.

BINDING

Cutting

From **BLACK PRINT**:
• Cut 4, 2-3/4 x 42-inch strips

Diagonally piece the strips as needed. Sew the binding to the quilt using a 3/8-inch seam allowance. This measurement will produce a 1/2-inch wide finished double binding. Read through **Binding** instructions on page 119 for complete instructions.

TIP . . . .

When hanging small quilts, use straight pins (this will be possible only if your walls are made of sheet rock). Place pin between the quilt and binding and tap lightly with a hammer in all four corners of your quilt.

Fabrics and Supplies

for queen bed with a 13-inch drop

*5 yards **Fabric** for dust ruffle*
3-3/4 yards Muslin for center panel
Quilting thread or cording for gathering the top edge of the dust ruffle

Special Measuring Instructions

If your drop length differs from 13-inches, use the following instructions to determine the correct drop length of your dust ruffle.

Step 1

Measure from the top edge of the box spring to the floor, and add 2-1/2-inches to allow for a hem and seam allowance.

Step 2

For ease in construction, make the dust ruffle in 3 sections - 2 for the sides and one for the foot end. To determine the number of fabric strips to cut for the dust ruffle, measure the side of your box spring and multiply this length by 2 or 2-1/2, depending on the fullness you want and the weight of your fabric. Repeat for the other side and the foot end of the bed. Add these measurements together to get the total inches needed.

Step 3

Cut and piece the strips of fabric according to the measurements determined in Steps 1 and 2.

Center Panel

Step 1

Cut the 3-3/4 yard length of muslin in half crosswise to make 2, 1-7/8 yard lengths. Sew the long edges together, and press. Trim the muslin to 61 x 80-3/4-inches.

Note: If your mattress size differs from 60 x 78-inches, measure the width and length of the bed's box spring. Add 1-inch to the width measurement and 2-3/4-inches to the length measurement to allow for a hem and seam allowance. Cut a piece of muslin according to this measurement to make the center panel.

Step 2

Turn one short edge of the muslin under 1/4-inch, and press. Turn the same edge under another 2-inches, and press. Stitch the folded edge in place to hem the top edge of the center panel.

Step 3

Measure the side of the center panel, from point A to point B. Divide the measurement by 4 and mark those points on the side raw edges of the center panel. Repeat for the other side (point C to point D) and the foot end (point B to point C).

Make the Dust Ruffle

Note: For ease in construction, make the dust ruffle in 3 sections - 2 for the sides and one for the foot end.

Cutting

From **Dust Ruffle** fabric:
- Cut 8, 15-1/2 x 42-inch strips. Piece 4 of the strips together for each side.
- Cut 3 more 15-1/2 x 42-inch strips. Piece the strips together for the foot end.

Piecing

Step 1

Working with one side section, turn a long edge of the dust ruffle under 1-inch, and press. Turn the same edge under

another 1-inch, and press. Stitch the folded edge in place to hem the lower edge. Make a 1-inch double hem for each short edge. Divide the top edge of the dust ruffle into fourths and mark with safety pins. Press, sew, and mark the remaining side section and foot end section in the same manner.

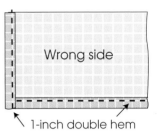

Step 2

To gather the dust ruffle, position 2 strands of quilting thread 1/4-inch from the raw edge. The length of the thread for each side section should be 160-inches long and 120-inches long for the foot end section. To gather the fabric, zigzag-stitch over the length of thread, pushing the fabric onto the thread as you continue stitching.

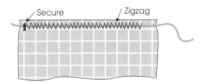

Step 3

With right sides together, and raw edges aligned, place a dust ruffle section on the center panel, matching marks and pin, referring to the diagram. Pull the thread to gather the dust ruffle into an even fit and pin in place. Sew the dust ruffle section to the center panel with a 1/2-inch seam allowance. Repeat to sew the remaining sections to the center panel to complete the dust ruffle.

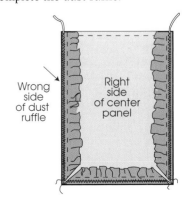

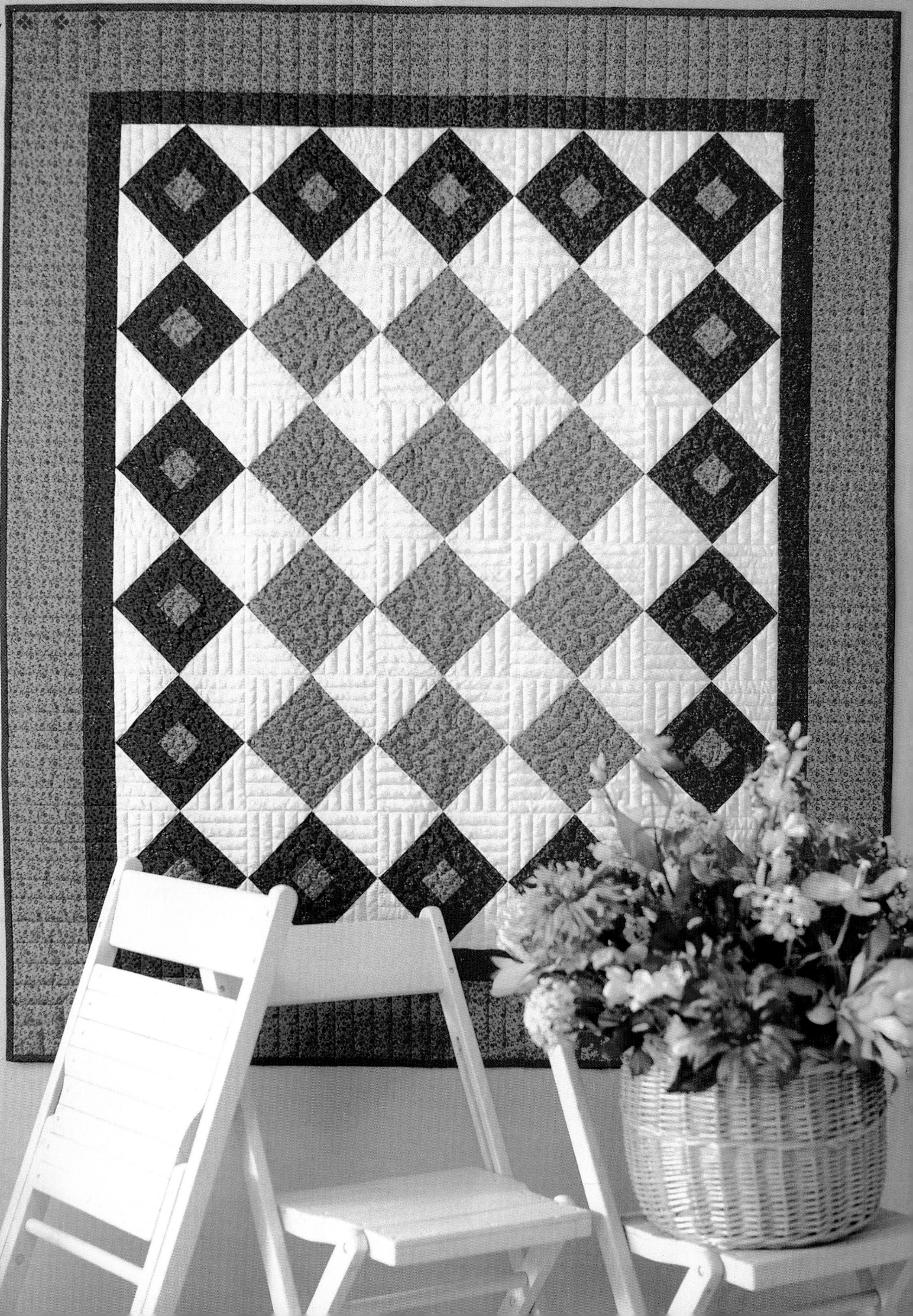

BLUEBERRY PATCH

Yardage is based on 42-inch wide fabric.

FABRICS AND SUPPLIES

1-1/4	yards	**DARK BLUE PRINT** for pieced blocks and inner border
1-3/4	yards	**LIGHT BLUE PRINT** for center blocks, pieced blocks, and outer border
1-1/2	yards	**BEIGE PRINT** for alternate blocks, side and corner triangles
5/8	yard	**BLUE GRID** for binding
3-1/3	yards	Backing fabric

Quilt batting, at least 60 x 69-inches

A rotary cutter, mat, and wide clear plastic ruler with 1/8-inch markings are needed tools in attaining accuracy. A 6 x 24-inch ruler and 12-1/2-inch acrylic square are recommended.

Blueberry Patch is an easy quilt to make because the majority of the blocks are not pieced. Only the outside row of blocks are pieced. Choose a large print fabric to do the design work for you. This pattern is a particularly good choice for flannels or novelty prints and can be finished by hand-quilting, machine-quilting, or perhaps tying.

56 x 65-inches
Block: 6-inches square

GETTING STARTED

❖ Read instructions thoroughly before beginning project.

❖ Prewash and press fabrics to test for color fastness and possible shrinkage.

❖ For piecing, place right sides of fabric pieces together and use 1/4-inch seam allowances throughout unless otherwise specified.

❖ It is very important that accurate 1/4-inch seam allowances are used. It is wise to stitch a sample 1/4-inch seam allowance to check your machine's seam allowance accuracy.

❖ Press seam allowances in one direction toward the darker fabric and/or in the direction that will create the least bulk.

❖ Instructions are given for quick cutting and piecing of blocks. Note that for some of the pieces, the quick-cutting method will result in leftover fabric.

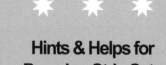

Hints & Helps for Pressing Strip Sets

When sewing strips of fabric together for strip sets, it is important to press the seam allowances nice and flat, usually to the dark fabric. Be careful not to stretch as you press, causing a "rainbow effect." This will affect the accuracy and shape of the pieces cut from the strip set. Press on the wrong side first with the strips perpendicular to the ironing board. Flip the piece over and press on the right side to prevent little pleats from forming at the seams. Laying the strip set lengthwise on the ironing board seems to encourage the rainbow effect, as shown in diagram.

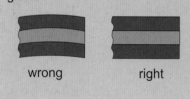

wrong   right

TIP . . . .

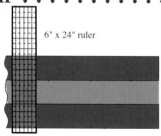

6" x 24" ruler

Make a habit of stopping often to check that your ruler is perpendicular to the strip set as you crosscut your segments. Lining up a horizontal marking on your ruler with a strip set seam will help keep your 2-1/2-inch segments "square."

PIECED BLOCKS

MAKE 18 BLOCKS

Note: To make the piecing easier for this block, we are using the strip piecing technique. This usually means there will be extra pieces of fabric remaining for fun small projects, or to save for pieced scrap borders. Read **Hints and Helps for Pressing Strip Sets**.

Cutting

From **DARK BLUE PRINT**:
- Cut 6, 2-1/2 x 42-inch strips. From these strips cut:
     36, 2-1/2 x 6-1/2-inch rectangles
- Cut 4 more 2-1/2 x 42-inch strips

From **LIGHT BLUE PRINT**:
- Cut 2, 2-1/2 x 42-inch strips

Piecing

Step 1

Aligning long edges, sew 2-1/2 x 42-inch **DARK BLUE** strips to both sides of the 2-1/2 x 42-inch **LIGHT BLUE** strips and press. Make a total of 2 strip sets. Cut the strip sets into segments.

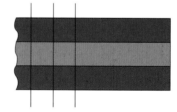

Crosscut 18,
2-1/2-inch
wide segments

Step 2

Sew 2-1/2 x 6-1/2-inch **DARK BLUE** rectangles to both sides of the Step 1 segments and press. <u>At this point each block should measure 6-1/2-inches square</u>.

Make 18

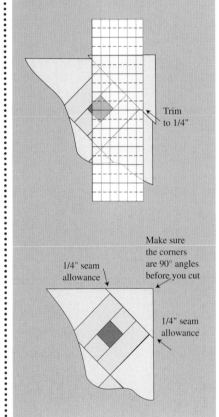

Trimming Side and Corner Triangles

❖ Begin at a corner by lining up your ruler 1/4-inch beyond the points of the corners of the blocks as shown. Cut along the edge of the ruler. Repeat this procedure on all four sides of the quilt top.

Trim to 1/4"

Make sure the corners are 90° angles before you cut

1/4" seam allowance

1/4" seam allowance

Quilt Center

Cutting

From **BEIGE PRINT**:
- Cut 4, 6-1/2 x 42-inch strips. From these strips cut:
    20, 6-1/2-inch squares for the alternate blocks
- Cut 2, 10-1/2 x 42-inch strips. From these strips cut:
    5, 10-1/2-inch squares. Cut each square twice diagonally to make 20 triangles. You will be using only 18 for side triangles. Also cut, 2, 6-1/2-inch squares. Cut each square once diagonally to make 4 corner triangles.

From **LIGHT BLUE PRINT**:
- Cut 2, 6-1/2 x 42-inch strips. From these strips cut:
    12, 6-1/2-inch center block squares

Diagonal Cutting Diagram

10-1/2-inch square

Side triangles

6-1/2-inch square

Corner triangles

Note: The side and corner triangles are larger than necessary and will be trimmed before the borders are added.

Quilt Center Assembly

Step 1

Referring to the quilt center diagram, sew together the 18 pieced blocks, alternate blocks, center blocks, and side triangles in 10 diagonal rows. Press the seam allowances in alternating directions by rows so the seams will fit snugly together with less bulk.

Quilt Center Assembly

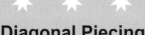

Diagonal Piecing

❖ For borders that are longer than 42-inches, piece the border strips together with diagonal seams. They are less visible in a finished quilt than straight seams.

❖ To sew two border strips together diagonally, place them together at a 90° angle with right sides together, as shown below.

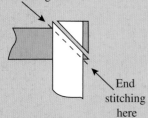

Begin stitching here

End stitching here

Each strip should extend approximately 1/4-inch beyond the other. Draw a diagonal line to use as your stitching guide. Sew the two strips together, taking care to start and stop your stitching precisely at the point where the two strips meet, as shown above. Trim away the excess fabric, leaving a 1/4-inch seam allowance, and press the seam open.

❖ Cut enough border strips so after your strips are stitched together, the diagonal seams will not be at the corners of the quilt top.

Step 2
Pin the rows at the block intersections, and sew the rows together. Press the row seams in one direction.

Step 3
Sew the corner triangles to the quilt and press.

Step 4
Trim away the excess fabric from the side and corner triangles taking care to allow a 1/4-inch seam allowance beyond the corners of each block. Read through **Trimming Side and Corner Triangles** on page 67 for complete instructions.

BORDERS

Note: The yardage given allows for the border strips to be cut on the crosswise grain. Diagonally piece the strips as needed. Read through **Borders** on page 118 for general instructions on adding borders.

Cutting

From **DARK BLUE PRINT**:
- Cut 5, 2-1/2 x 42-inch inner border strips

From **LIGHT BLUE PRINT**:
- Cut 7, 5-1/2 x 42-inch outer border strips

Attaching the Borders

Refer to Border Assembly Diagram on page 17.

Step 1
Attach the 2-1/2-inch wide **DARK BLUE** inner border strips.

Step 2
Attach the 5-1/2-inch wide **LIGHT BLUE** outer border strips.

QUILTING DESIGNS . . . .

Quilting suggestions
for quilt blocks

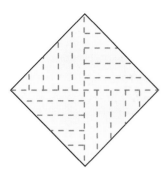

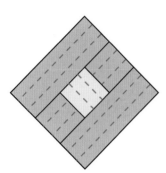

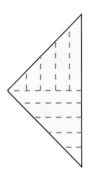

Border Assembly Diagram

PUTTING IT ALL TOGETHER

Cut the 3-1/3 yard length of backing fabric in half crosswise to make 2,
1-2/3 yard lengths. Read through **Finishing the Quilt** on page 118 for
complete instructions.

BINDING

Cutting

From **BLUE GRID**:
• Cut 7, 2-3/4 x 42-inch strips

Diagonally piece the strips as needed. Sew the binding to the quilt using a
3/8-inch seam allowance. This measurement will produce a 1/2-inch wide
finished double binding. Read through **Binding** instructions on page 119
for complete instructions.

BUILDING BLOCKS
LITTLE GIRL COLORS

Yardage is based on 42-inch wide fabric.

FABRICS AND SUPPLIES

1/4 yard **each of 5 COORDINATING PRINTS**
    for block rows

3/4 yard **BEIGE PRINT** for background

7/8 yard **GREEN PRINT** for lattice strips, inner border,
    and corner square units

1/4 yard **PLUM PRINT** for corner square units

3/4 yard **PINK FLORAL** for outer border

1/2 yard **GOLD PRINT** for binding

2-3/4 yards Backing fabric

Quilt batting, at least 48 x 64-inches

A rotary cutter, mat, and wide clear plastic ruler
with 1/8-inch markings are needed tools in attaining
accuracy. A 6 x 24-inch ruler and 12-1/2-inch
acrylic square are recommended.

*Many new quilters are tempted to make
a baby quilt as one of their first quilting
projects. This quilt design is simple and
graphic and it is easy enough to change
the colors to make a little boy version.
You will fall back on this quilt pattern
often.*

44 x 60-inches
Block: 4-inches square

GETTING STARTED

❖ Read instructions thoroughly before beginning project.
❖ Prewash and press fabrics to test for color fastness and
    possible shrinkage.
❖ For piecing, place right sides of fabric pieces together
    and use 1/4-inch seam allowances throughout unless
    otherwise specified.
❖ It is very important that accurate 1/4-inch seam
    allowances are used. It is wise to stitch a sample 1/4-inch
    seam allowance to check your machine's seam
    allowance accuracy.
❖ Press seam allowances in one direction toward the
    darker fabric and/or in the direction that will create the
    least bulk.
❖ Instructions are given for quick cutting and piecing of
    blocks. Note that for some of the pieces, the quick-
    cutting method will result in leftover fabric.

Tip . . . .

Make a habit of stopping often to check that your ruler is perpendicular to the strip set as you crosscut your segments. Lining up a horizontal marking on your ruler with a strip set seam will help keep your 4-1/2-inch segments square.

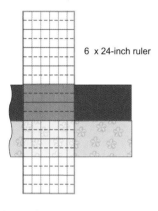

6 x 24-inch ruler

Tip . . . .

Pressing directions are indicated with arrows.

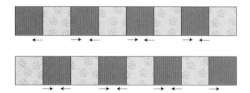

BLOCK ROWS

MAKE 5 BLOCK ROWS

Cutting

From **each** of the **5 COORDINATING PRINTS:**
• Cut 1, 4-1/2 x 42-inch strip

From **BEIGE PRINT:**
• Cut 5, 4-1/2 x 42-inch strips

Piecing

Step 1

Aligning long edges, sew each of the **5 COORDINATING PRINT** strips to a 4-1/2 x 42-inch **BEIGE** strip. Press the seam allowances toward the **COORDINATING PRINT** strips. Make a total of 5 strip sets. Cut **each** of the strip sets into segments.

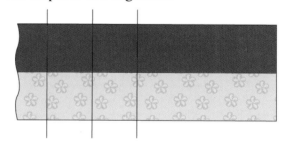

Crosscut **each** of the
strip sets into 8,
4-1/2-inch wide segments

Step 2

Referring to the diagram, sew the 8 segments together for each block row and press. <u>At this point each block row should measure 8-1/2 x 32-1/2-inches</u>.

Make a total of 5 block rows

Perfect Block Alignment

❖ By taking care to carefully pin your quilt top, you can achieve perfectly aligned block rows with little effort. Starting with your bottom pieced block row, with lattice already attached, lay the next block row (right sides together) over the previous row, making sure to line up seams of each block row. Adjust seams if necessary or ease fabric between seams to keep all vertical seam lines straight. Use the straight edge of your clear acrylic ruler to aid in seam alignment and pin often to keep seams from shifting. This will result in a perfectly pieced quilt.

QUILT CENTER AND INNER BORDER

Cutting

From **GREEN PRINT**:
• Cut 9, 2-1/2 x 42-inch strips. From these strips cut:
  6, 2-1/2 x 32-1/2-inch lattice strips and top/bottom inner border strips.
The remaining strips will be used for the side inner border strips. Diagonally piece the strips as needed, referring to page 22 for **Diagonal Piecing** instructions.

Quilt Center Assembly

Step 1
Referring to the quilt diagram, sew together the 5 block rows and the 6, 2-1/2 x 32-1/2-inch **GREEN** lattice and top/bottom inner border strips. Press the seam allowance toward the **GREEN** lattice strips.

Step 2
To attach the 2-1/2-inch wide **GREEN** side inner border strips, measure the quilt from top to bottom through the middle. Measure and mark the border lengths and center points on the 2-1/2-inch wide **GREEN** strips. Pin the border strips to the quilt; stitch and press. Trim away the excess fabric.

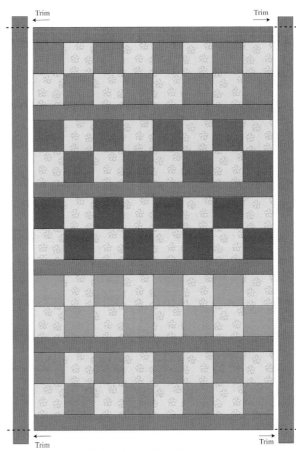

Quilt Assembly Diagram

Diagonal Piecing

❖ For borders that are longer than 42-inches, piece the border strips together with diagonal seams. They are less visible in a finished quilt than straight seams.

❖ To sew two border strips together diagonally, place them together at a 90° angle with right sides together, as shown below.

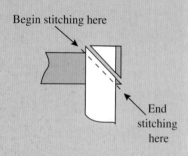

Begin stitching here

End stitching here

Each strip should extend approximately 1/4-inch beyond the other. Draw a diagonal line to use as your stitching guide. Sew the two strips together, taking care to start and stop your stitching precisely at the point where the two strips meet, as shown above. Trim away the excess fabric, leaving a 1/4-inch seam allowance, and press the seam open.

❖ Cut enough border strips, so after your strips are stitched together, the diagonal seams will not be at the corners of the quilt top.

OUTER BORDER

Note: The yardage given allows for the border strips to be cut on the crosswise grain. Diagonally piece the strips as needed, referring to **Diagonal Piecing** instructions.

Cutting

From **PINK FLORAL**:
- Cut 5, 4-1/2 x 42-inch outer border strips

From **PLUM PRINT**:
- Cut 1, 4-1/2 x 42-inch strip. From this strip cut:
     8, 4-1/2-inch corner squares

From **GREEN PRINT**:
- Cut 4, 4-1/2-inch corner squares

Assembling and Attaching the Border

Step 1
To make the top and bottom outer borders, measure the quilt from left to right through the middle. A 4-1/2-inch **PLUM** square will be added to both ends of each **PINK FLORAL** outer border strip; therefore, subtract a total of 8-inches from the measurement taken above. Cut 2, 4-1/2-inch wide **PINK FLORAL** outer border strips to this length and sew 4-1/2-inch **PLUM** squares to both ends of the 2 strips. Sew the pieced outer border strips to the top and bottom of the quilt and press.

Step 2
Sew the remaining 4-1/2-inch **PLUM** squares to the 4-1/2-inch **GREEN** squares and press. At this point each corner square unit should measure 4-1/2 x 8-1/2-inches.

Make 4 corner square units

Step 3
To make the side outer borders, measure the quilt from top to bottom through the middle including the borders just added. The Step 2 corner square units will be added to both ends of each **PINK FLORAL** outer border strip; therefore, subtract a total of 16-inches from the measurement taken above. Cut 2, 4-1/2-inch wide **PINK FLORAL** outer border strips to this length and sew Step 2 corner square units to both ends of the 2 strips. Sew the pieced outer border strips to the quilt and press.

PUTTING IT ALL TOGETHER

Cut the 2-3/4 yard length of backing fabric in half crosswise to make 2, 1-3/8 yard lengths. Refer to **Finishing the Quilt** on page 118 for complete instructions.

BINDING

Cutting

From **GOLD PRINT:**
• Cut 6, 2-3/4 x 42-inch strips

Sew the binding to the quilt using a 3/8-inch seam allowance. This measurement will produce a 1/2-inch wide finished double binding. Refer to **Binding** and **Diagonal Piecing** instructions on page 119 for complete instructions.

Building Blocks - Little Boy Colors
44 x 60-inches
Block: 4-inches square

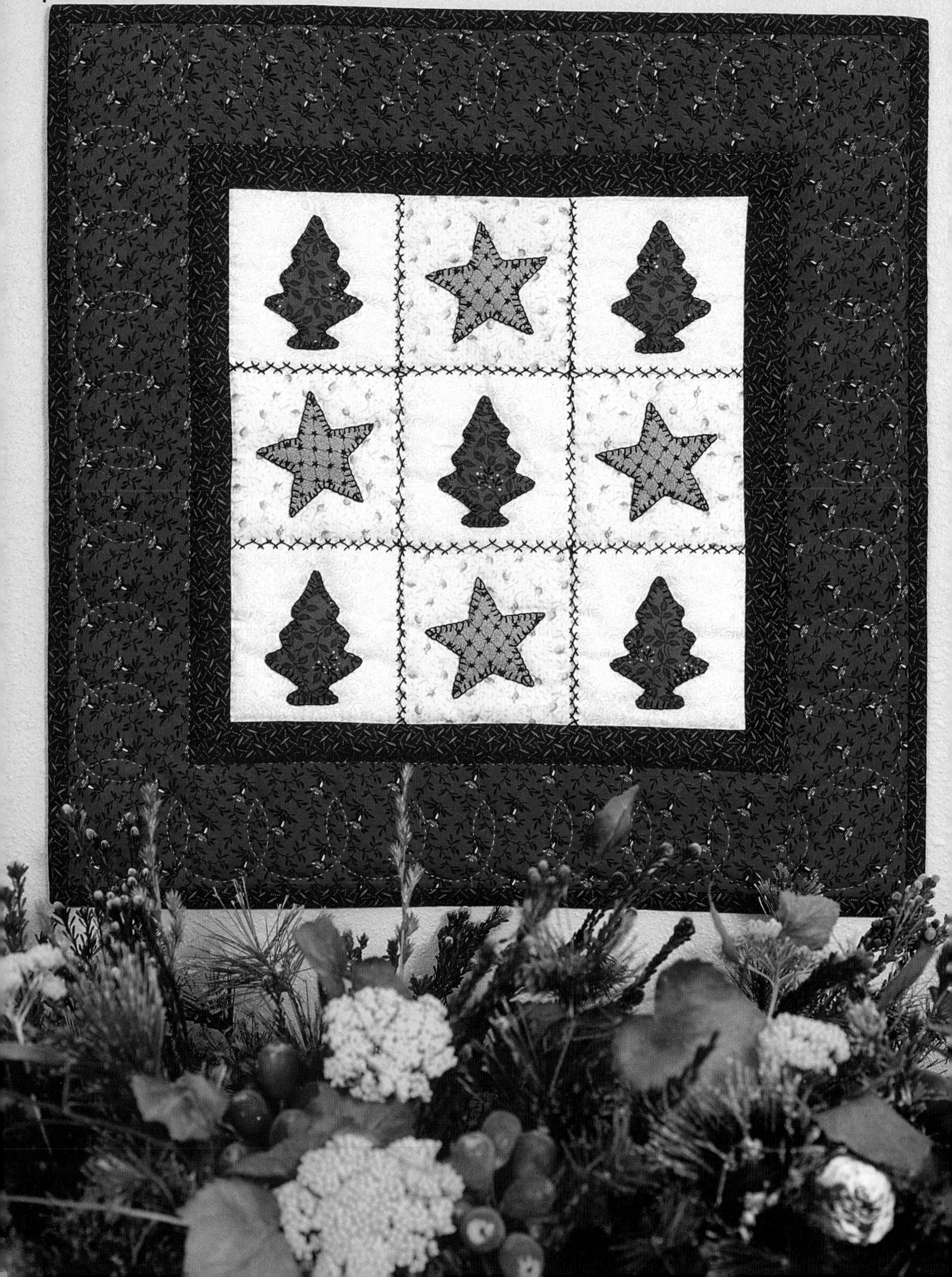

CHRISTMAS TIC-TAC-TOE

Yardage is based on 42-inch wide fabric.

FABRICS AND SUPPLIES

1/4	yard	**BEIGE PRINT #1** for applique foundation
1/4	yard	**BEIGE PRINT #2** for applique foundation
1/8	yard	**GREEN PRINT** for tree appliques
1/8	yard	**GOLD PRINT** for star appliques
1/8	yard	**BLACK PRINT** for inner border
1/4	yard	**RED PRINT** for outer border
1/4	yard	**BLACK PRINT** for binding
1/3	yard	Paper-backed fusible web for appliques

#8 Black pearl cotton for decorative stitches

2/3	yard	Backing fabric

Quilt batting, at least 24-inches square

A rotary cutter, mat, and wide clear plastic ruler with 1/8-inch markings are needed tools in attaining accuracy. A 6 x 24-inch ruler and 12-1/2-inch acrylic square are recommended.

This wonderful little wall quilt is so fun and easy to make that it just might become your holiday gift to everyone on your list. With just a few small scraps of leftover fabric, you are well on your way to making more than one. The appliques are fused on with an iron and decorative stitches are added as an option to make it even more special.

20-inches square
Block: 4-inches square

GETTING STARTED

❖ Read instructions thoroughly before beginning project.

❖ Prewash and press fabrics to test for color fastness and possible shrinkage.

❖ For piecing, place right sides of fabric pieces together and use 1/4-inch seam allowances throughout unless otherwise specified.

❖ It is very important that accurate 1/4-inch seam allowances are used. It is wise to stitch a sample 1/4-inch seam allowance to check your machine's seam allowance accuracy.

❖ Press seam allowances in one direction toward the darker fabric and/or in the direction that will create the least bulk.

❖ Instructions are given for quick cutting and piecing of blocks. Note that for some of the pieces, the quick-cutting method will result in leftover fabric.

PRESHRINKING SMALL AMOUNTS OF FABRIC

To test for color fastness and to preshrink small pieces, place them on a piece of muslin on your ironing board. Dampen and iron dry. This will preshrink the fabric and it will also indicate if the fabric is going to bleed.

TIPS . . . .

If you're trying to decide between using the pearl cotton and the embroidery floss, consider this: Pearl cotton is a bit thicker and has more sheen than embroidery floss. Your buttonhole stitches will be more noticeable with the pearl cotton.

_____

To prevent the buttonhole-stitches from "rolling off" the edges of the appliques, take an extra back-stitch in the same place as you made the buttonhole-stitch, going around outer curves, corners, and points. For straight edges, taking a back-stitch every inch is enough.

_____

To personalize this quilt for other seasons or special celebrations, use cookie cutters for a great variety of different applique shapes. Simply trace the cutter shape onto the fusible web following our applique instructions.

APPLIQUE BLOCKS
Make 5 tree blocks
Make 4 star blocks

Cutting

From **BEIGE PRINT #1:**
- Cut 1, 4-1/2 x 42-inch strip. From this strip cut:
    5, 4-1/2-inch squares

From **BEIGE PRINT #2:**
- Cut 1, 4-1/2 x 42-inch strip. From this strip cut:
    4, 4-1/2-inch squares

Fusible Web Applique

Step 1
Position the fusible web, paper side up, over the applique shapes. With a pencil, trace the shapes the number of times as indicated on each pattern, leaving a small margin between each shape. Cut the shapes apart.

Step 2
Following the manufacturer's instructions, fuse the shapes to the wrong side of the fabrics chosen for the appliques. Let the fabric cool and cut along the traced line. Peel away the paper backing from the fusible web.

Step 3
Referring to the quilt diagram, center the fused applique shapes onto the applique foundation squares and press with a dry iron.

Step 4
Using black pearl cotton, buttonhole-stitch the tree and star shapes in place.

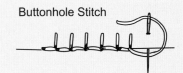

Buttonhole Stitch

QUILT CENTER

Step 1
Referring to the quilt diagram, sew the tree and star blocks together in 3 rows of 3 blocks each. Press the seam allowances open.

Step 2
Pin the rows at the block intersections and sew the rows together. Press the seam rows open.

Freezer Paper Applique

Trace the applique shapes onto the paper side of the freezer paper. Cut out the shapes on the drawn lines. With a hot iron, press the shapes to the wrong side of the designated fabrics, allowing at least 1/2-inch between each shape for seam allowances. Cut out each shape a scant 1/4-inch beyond the edge of the freezer paper pattern to allow for a seam allowance.

It may be easier to applique the shapes if you first hand-baste the pieces onto the quilt top. This will avoid catching your thread on the pins.

Hold the block to be appliqued with your non-sewing hand. Use the side of the needle's point to turn under the seam allowance. Hold the turned under edge with your thumbnail as you stitch the shape in place.

To make your applique stitches, use a matching thread color. Start appliqueing by coming up through the backside of the quilt and catch the edge of the applique shape with your needle. Go back straight down through the quilt and come back up for the next stitch, about 1/16th of an inch away from the previous stitch.

Using size 10 or 11 straw needles gives your applique a great look. They are extra long and flexible and will be easier to guide through the fabric.

Step 3

Using black pearl cotton, herringbone-stitch over the seam lines. Use the open seam allowances as a placement guideline for the herringbone stitches. You will be able to feel the edges of the seams.

Herringbone Stitch

BORDERS

Note: *The yardage given allows for the border strips to be cut on the crosswise grain. Read through* **Border** *instructions on page 118 for general instructions on adding borders.*

Cutting

From **BLACK PRINT:**
- Cut 2, 1-1/2 x 42-inch inner border strips

From **RED PRINT:**
- Cut 2, 3-1/2 x 42-inch outer border strips

Attaching the Borders

Step 1

Attach the 1-1/2-inch wide **BLACK** inner border strips.

Step 2

Attach the 3-1/2-inch wide **RED** outer border strips.

Border Assembly Diagram

TIP . . . .

When hanging small quilts, use straight pins (this will be possible only if your walls are made of sheet rock). Place pin between the quilt and binding and tap lightly with a hammer in all four corners of your quilt.

PUTTING IT ALL TOGETHER

Trim the backing and batting so they are 4-inches larger than the quilt top. Refer to **Finishing the Quilt** on page 118 for complete instructions.

BINDING

Cutting

From **BLACK PRINT:**
- Cut 3, 2-3/4 x 42-inch strips

Sew the binding to the quilt using a 3/8-inch seam allowance. This measurement will produce a 1/2-inch wide finished double binding. Refer to **Binding** and **Diagonal Piecing** instructions on page 119 for complete instructions.

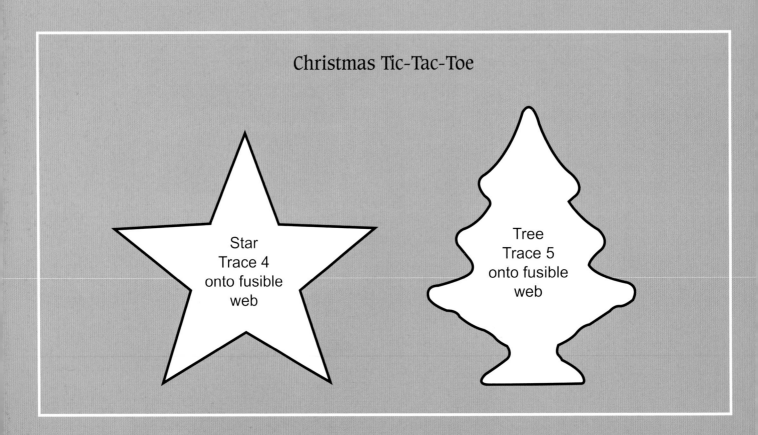

Christmas Tic-Tac-Toe

Star
Trace 4
onto fusible
web

Tree
Trace 5
onto fusible
web

Quilt Name

Made By

Date

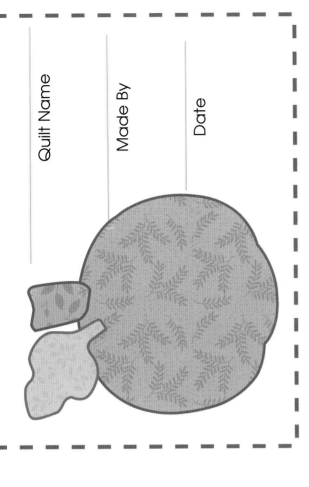

Quilt Name

Made By

Date

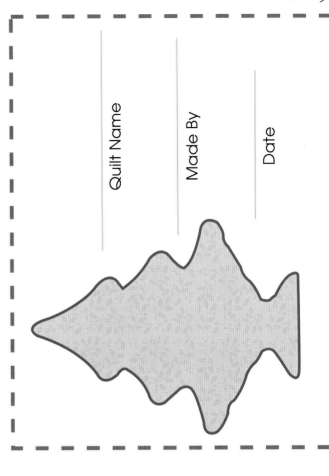

Quilt Label Artwork - Trace shapes onto fusible web. Fuse to a piece of light colored fabric. Document quilt using a permanent marking pencil. Turn raw edges of quilt label under 1/4" and stitch to the back of the quilt

Quilt Name

Made By

Date

Quilt Name

Made By

Date

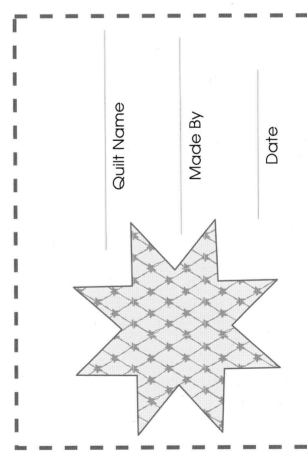

DOWNHILL

Yardage is based on 42-inch wide fabric.

FABRICS AND SUPPLIES

7/8	yard	**GREEN PRINT #1** for trees
1-1/8	yards	**BEIGE PRINT #1** for tree background
1/4	yard	**BROWN PRINT** for tree trunks
7/8	yard	**BLUE PRINT** for triangle blocks
7/8	yard	**BEIGE PRINT #2** for triangle blocks
3	yards	**CHESTNUT PRINT** for lattice segments and corner squares
1-1/4	yards	**GREEN PRINT #2** for lattice posts and corner triangles
1-3/4	yards	**RED PRINT** for border
1-1/8	yards	**RED PLAID** for binding (cut on the bias)
6	yards	Backing fabric

Quilt batting, at least 80 x 104-inches

A rotary cutter, mat, and wide clear plastic ruler with 1/8-inch markings are needed tools in attaining accuracy. A 6 x 24-inch ruler and 12-1/2-inch acrylic square are recommended.

76 x 100-inches
Block: 8-inches square

GETTING STARTED

❖ Read instructions thoroughly before beginning project.

❖ Prewash and press fabrics to test for color fastness and possible shrinkage.

❖ For piecing, place right sides of fabric pieces together and use 1/4-inch seam allowances throughout unless otherwise specified.

❖ It is very important that accurate 1/4-inch seam allowances are used. It is wise to stitch a sample 1/4-inch seam allowance to check your machine's seam allowance accuracy.

❖ Press seam allowances in one direction toward the darker fabric and/or in the direction that will create the least bulk.

❖ Instructions are given for quick cutting and piecing of blocks. Note that for some of the pieces, the quick-cutting method will result in leftover fabric.

TIP . . . .

Stitch on the outer edge just a "hair" or a thread width from the marked diagonal line.

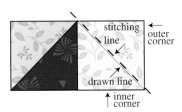

If you stitch on the inner corner side of the diagonal line you will actually make the triangle smaller.

Hints & Helps for Chain Piecing

To make the piecing process for "Downhill" more efficient, plan on chain piecing all of the left-hand "triangles" at one time. Clip, trim, and press; then repeat on the right-hand side of the rectangle.

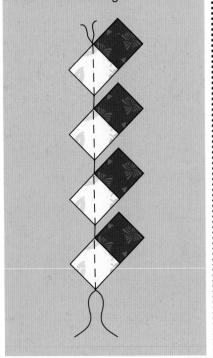

TREE BLOCKS

MAKE 18 BLOCKS

Cutting

From **GREEN PRINT #1:**
• Cut 11, 2-1/2 x 42-inch strips. From these strips cut:
   36, 2-1/2 x 8-1/2-inch rectangles
   18, 2-1/2 x 4-1/2-inch rectangles

From **BEIGE PRINT #1:**
• Cut 9, 2-1/2 x 42-inch strips. From these strips cut:
   144, 2-1/2-inch squares
• Cut 4, 3-1/2 x 42-inch strips

From **BROWN PRINT:**
• Cut 2, 2-1/2 x 42-inch strips

Piecing

Step 1

Position a 2-1/2-inch **BEIGE** square on the left side of a 2-1/2 x 4-1/2-inch **GREEN** rectangle. Draw a diagonal line on the square and stitch on the line. Trim the seam allowance to 1/4-inch and press. Repeat this process at the opposite side of the rectangle. Sew 2-1/2-inch **BEIGE** squares to the side edges of each unit and press. <u>At this point each unit should measure 2-1/2 x 8-1/2-inches</u>.

Make 18   Make 18

Step 2

Position a 2-1/2-inch **BEIGE** square on both sides of a 2-1/2 x 8-1/2-inch **GREEN** rectangle. Draw a diagonal line on each square, stitch, trim, and press. <u>At this point each unit should measure 2-1/2 x 8-1/2-inches</u>.

Make 36

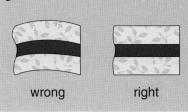
TIP . . . .

A 12-1/2-inch square acrylic ruler is great for squaring up individual blocks and corners of a quilt top, for cutting strips up to 12-1/2-inches wide or long, and for trimming side and corner triangles.

Step 3

To make the trunk units, sew a 3-1/2 x 42-inch **BEIGE** strip to both sides of a 2-1/2 x 42-inch **BROWN** strip and press toward the dark strip. Make 2 strip sets. Cut the strip sets into segments.

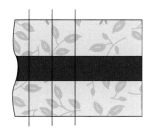

Crosscut 18, 2-1/2-inch wide segments

Step 4

Referring to the block diagram, sew the Step 1, 2, and 3 units together and press. <u>At this point each tree block should measure 8-1/2-inches square.</u>

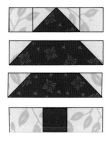
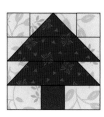

Make 18

TRIANGLE BLOCKS

MAKE 17 BLOCKS

Cutting

From **BLUE PRINT:**
- Cut 3, 8-7/8 x 42-inch strips. From these strips cut:
    9, 8-7/8-inch squares

From **BEIGE PRINT #2:**
- Cut 3, 8-7/8 x 42-inch strips. From these strips cut:
    9, 8-7/8-inch squares

Piecing

With right sides together, layer the 8-7/8-inch **BLUE** and **BEIGE #2** squares in pairs. Press together, but do not sew. Cut the layered squares in half diagonally to make 17 sets of triangles. (You will have one triangle set left over.) Stitch 1/4-inch from the diagonal edge of each pair of triangles and press toward the **BLUE** triangle. <u>At this point each triangle block should measure 8-1/2-inches square.</u>

TIP . . . .

Pressing the layered squares together before cutting them diagonally prevents the fabric from shifting and makes it easier to be more accurate.

Layer the **BLUE** and **BEIGE** squares right sides together <u>before</u> cutting.

 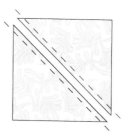 

Make 17, 8-1/2-inch
triangle blocks

QUILT CENTER

Cutting

From **CHESTNUT PRINT**:
- Cut 21, 4-1/2 x 42-inch strips. From these strips cut:
    - 82, 4-1/2 x 8-1/2-inch lattice segments

From **GREEN PRINT #2**:
- Cut 6, 4-1/2 x 42-inch strips. From these strips cut:
    - 48, 4-1/2-inch lattice post squares

Quilt Center Assembly

Step 1
Referring to the diagram, sew together 5 of the 4-1/2 x 8-1/2-inch **CHESTNUT** lattice segments and 6 of the 4-1/2-inch **GREEN #2** lattice posts. Press the seam allowances toward the **CHESTNUT** lattice segments. <u>At this point each lattice strip should measure 4-1/2 x 64-1/2-inches.</u>

Make 8 lattice strips

Step 2
Referring to the quilt center assembly diagram for block placement, sew together the tree blocks, triangle blocks, and 4-1/2 x 8-1/2-inch **CHESTNUT** lattice segments to make 7 block rows. Press the seam allowances toward the **CHESTNUT** lattice segments. <u>At this point each block row should measure 8-1/2 x 64-1/2-inches.</u>

TIP . . . .

Pressing directions
are indicated with arrows.

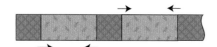

Diagonal Piecing

❖ For borders that are longer than 42-inches, piece the border strips together with diagonal seams. They are less visible in a finished quilt than straight seams.

❖ To sew two border strips together diagonally, place them together at a 90 degree angle with right sides together, as shown below.

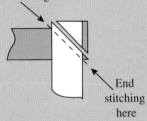

Begin stitching here

End stitching here

Each strip should extend approximately 1/4-inch beyond the other. Draw a diagonal line to use as your stitching guide. Sew the two strips together, taking care to start and stop your stitching precisely at the point where the two strips meet, as shown above. Trim away the excess fabric, leaving a 1/4-inch seam allowance, and press the seam open.

❖ Cut enough border strips, so after your strips are stitched together, the diagonal seams will not be at the corners of the quilt top.

Step 3

Referring to the quilt diagram, pin the block rows and lattice strips together at the block intersections and sew. Press the row seams toward the lattice strips. At this point the quilt center should measure 64-1/2 x 88-1/2-inches.

Quilt Center Assembly

BORDER

Note: The yardage given allows for the border strips to be cut on the crosswise grain. Diagonally piece the strips as needed, referring to **Diagonal Piecing** instructions. Read through **Borders** on page 118 for general instructions on adding borders.

Cutting

From **RED PRINT:**
- Cut 2, 6-1/2 x 88-1/2-inch side border strips
- Cut 2, 6-1/2 x 64-1/2-inch top/bottom border strips

From **GREEN PRINT #2**
- Cut 2, 6-1/2 x 42-inch strips. From these strips cut:
    8, 6-1/2-inch squares

From **CHESTNUT PRINT:**
- Cut 1, 6-1/2 x 42-inch strip. From this strip cut:
    4, 6-1/2-inch corner squares

Assembling and Attaching the Border

Step 1

Position a 6-1/2-inch **GREEN** square on both sides of a 6-1/2 x 64-1/2-inch **RED** border strip. Draw a diagonal line on each square and stitch on the line. Trim the seam allowance to 1/4-inch and press. <u>At this point each lattice strip should measure 6-1/2 x 64-1/2-inches.</u>

Make 2 border strips

Step 2

Sew the borders to the top and bottom edges of the quilt center and press.

QUILTING DESIGNS . . . .

Quilting suggestions
for quilt blocks and lattice

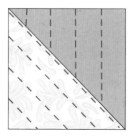

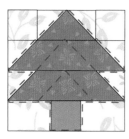

Border Assembly Diagram

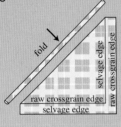

Step 3

Referring to the Step 1 diagram, position a 6-1/2-inch **GREEN** square on both sides of a 6-1/2 x 88-1/2-inch **RED** border strip. Draw a diagonal line on each square and stitch on the line. Trim the seam allowances to 1/4-inch and press. Referring to the quilt diagram, add the 6-1/2-inch **CHESTNUT** corner squares to both ends of the border strips and press. At this point each border strip should measure 6-1/2 x 100-1/2 inches. Make 2 border strips. Sew the borders to the quilt and press.

PUTTING IT ALL TOGETHER

Cut the 6 yard length of backing fabric in half crosswise to make 2, 3 yard lengths. Read through **Finishing the Quilt** on page 118 for complete instructions.

BINDING

Cutting

From **RED PLAID**:
- Cut enough 2-3/4-inch wide **bias** strips to make a 370-inch long strip.

Diagonally piece the strips as needed. Sew the binding to the quilt using a 3/8-inch seam allowance. This measurement will produce a 1/2-inch wide finished double binding. Read through **Binding** instructions on page 119 for complete instructions.

FOUR-PATCH NAPPER

Yardage is based on 42-inch wide fabric.

FABRICS AND SUPPLIES

3/4	yard	**RED PRINT #1** for blocks and lattice posts
1-2/3	yards	**BLUE PRINT** for four-patch blocks and border
1-2/3	yards	**BEIGE PRINT** for block background
1-1/4	yards	**GOLD PRINT** for lattice segments
2/3	yard	**RED PRINT #2** for binding
3-3/4	yards	Backing fabric

Quilt batting, at least 64 x 76-inches

A rotary cutter, mat, and wide clear plastic ruler with 1/8-inch markings are needed tools in attaining accuracy. A 6 x 24-inch ruler and 12-1/2-inch acrylic square are recommended.

This quilt is the perfect size for a couch throw or an accent on the bottom of a bed. This traditional patchwork design was often chosen as a way to use up scraps from other projects.

60 x 72-inches
Block: 9-1/4-inches square

GETTING STARTED

❖ Read instructions thoroughly before beginning project.

❖ Prewash and press fabrics to test for color fastness and possible shrinkage.

❖ For piecing, place right sides of fabric pieces together and use 1/4-inch seam allowances throughout unless otherwise specified.

❖ It is very important that accurate 1/4-inch seam allowances are used. It is wise to stitch a sample 1/4-inch seam allowance to check your machine's seam allowance accuracy.

❖ Press seam allowances in one direction toward the darker fabric and/or in the direction that will create the least bulk.

❖ Instructions are given for quick cutting and piecing of blocks. Note that for some of the pieces, the quick-cutting method will result in leftover fabric.

FOUR-PATCH BLOCKS

MAKE 20 BLOCKS

Cutting

From **RED PRINT #1**:
* Cut 4, 3-3/4 x 42-inch strips

From **BLUE PRINT**:
* Cut 4, 3-3/4 x 42-inch strips

From **BEIGE PRINT**:
* Cut 8, 7 x 42-inch strips. From these strips cut: 40, 7-inch squares, cutting each square once diagonally to make 80 corner triangles

Note: The **BEIGE PRINT** corner triangles are larger than necessary and will be trimmed before the lattice segments are added.

Piecing

Step 1
Aligning long edges, sew the 3-3/4 x 42-inch **RED** and **BLUE** strips together in pairs and press. Make a total of 4 strip sets. Cut the strip sets into segments.

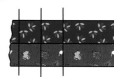

Crosscut 40,
3-3/4-inch wide
segments

Step 2
Sew the segments together in pairs and press. <u>At this point each four-patch block should measure 7-inches square.</u>

Make 20
four-patch blocks

Step 3
Center a **BEIGE** corner triangle on 2 opposite sides of a four-patch block. Stitch in place and press. Center **BEIGE** corner triangles on the remaining sides of the block, stitch in place, and press.

Make 20
blocks

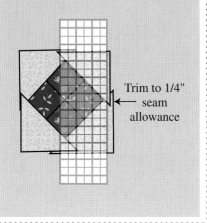

Trimming Corner Triangles

❖ Begin at a corner by lining up your ruler 1/4-inch beyond the points of the corners of the blocks as shown. Cut along the edge of the ruler. Repeat this procedure on all four sides of each block.

Trim to 1/4" seam allowance

TIP . . . .

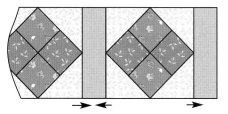

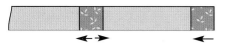

Pressing directions are indicated with arrows.

Step 4

Trim away the excess fabric from the corner triangles taking care to allow a 1/4-inch seam allowance beyond the corners of each block. Refer to **Trimming Corner Triangles** for complete instructions.

Note: Because the four-patch blocks are set on point, the finished block is not a typical block size. Therefore, it is necessary to measure your blocks at this point. All of your blocks need to be the same size, approximately 9-5/8-inches square. The **GOLD** lattice segments should be cut to match the block size.

QUILT CENTER

Cutting

From **GOLD PRINT**:
- Cut 13, 3 x 42-inch strips. From these strips cut:
  49 lattice segment rectangles, 3-inch wide x the block measurement taken in Step 4 (approximately 9-5/8-inches long)

From **RED PRINT #1**:
- Cut 3, 3 x 42-inch strips. From these strips cut:
  30, 3-inch lattice post squares

Quilt Center Assembly

Step 1

To make a block row, sew together 4 of the pieced four-patch blocks and 5 of the 3-inch wide **GOLD** lattice segments. Press the seam allowances toward the lattice segments.

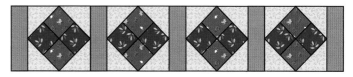

Make 5 block rows

Step 2

To make the lattice strips, sew together 4 of the 3-inch wide **GOLD** lattice segments and 5 of the 3-inch **RED** lattice posts. Press the seam allowances toward the lattice segments.

Make 6 lattice strips

Step 3

Pin the rows together at the block intersections and sew together. Press the row seams toward the lattice strips.

Quilt Assembly Diagram

Diagonal Piecing

❖ For borders that are longer than 42-inches, piece the border strips together with diagonal seams. They are less visible in a finished quilt than straight seams.

❖ To sew two border strips together diagonally, place them together at a 90° angle with right sides together, as shown below. Each strip should extend approximately 1/4-inch beyond the other. Draw a diagonal line to use as your stitching guide. Sew the two strips together, taking care to start and stop your stitching precisely at the point where the two strips meet, as shown below. Trim away the excess fabric, leaving a 1/4-inch seam allowance, and press the seam open.

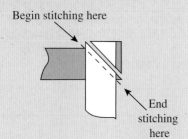

Begin stitching here

End stitching here

❖ Cut enough border strips so after your strips are stitched together, the diagonal seams will not be at the corners of the quilt top.

BORDER

Note: The yardage given allows for the border strips to be cut on the crosswise grain. Diagonally piece the strips as needed, referring to **Diagonal Piecing** instructions. Read through **Border** instructions on page 118 for general instructions on adding borders.

Cutting

From **BLUE PRINT**:
- Cut 7, 5-3/4 x 42-inch border strips

Attaching the Border

Attach the 5-3/4-inch wide **BLUE** border strips.

Border Assembly Diagram

Putting It All Together

Cut the 3-3/4 yard length of backing fabric in half crosswise to make 2, 1-7/8 yard lengths. Read through **Finishing the Quilt** on page 118 for complete instructions.

Binding

Cutting

From RED PRINT #2:
- Cut 7, 2-3/4 x 42-inch strips

Diagonally piece the strips as needed. Sew the binding to the quilt using a 3/8-inch seam allowance. This measurement will produce a 1/2-inch wide finished double binding. Read through **Binding** instructions on page 119 for complete instructions.

Just Around the Corner

Flannel Quilt

Yardage is based on 42-inch wide fabric.

Fabrics and Supplies

2-1/8	yards	**RED PRINT** for center rectangle and borders
7/8	yard	**GREEN SOLID** for borders
5/8	yard	**BEIGE PRINT** for border
3/4	yard	**GREEN PRINT** for border
1-3/8	yards	**RED PLAID** for binding (cut on the bias)
3-1/3	yards	Backing fabric

Quilt batting, at least 58 x 74-inches

A rotary cutter, mat, and wide clear plastic ruler with 1/8-inch markings are needed tools in attaining accuracy. A 6 x 24-inch ruler is recommended.

Kid's quilt, T.V. quilt, college quilt . . . Just Around the Corner is one of the fastest and easiest flannel quilts to make and works for any age group. For a scrappy look, make every border strip a different piece of coordinating flannel. It's a great way to use up leftover strips of flannel that you might have.

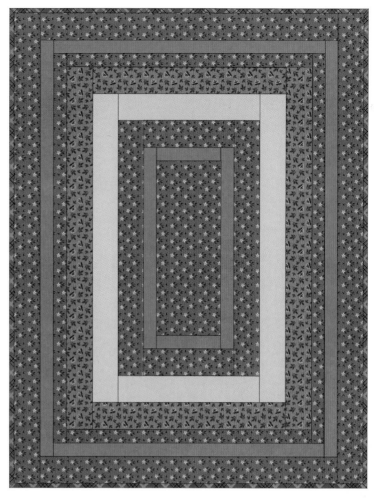

54 x 70-inches

Getting Started

❖ Read instructions thoroughly before beginning project.

❖ Prewash and press fabrics to test for color fastness and possible shrinkage.

❖ For piecing, place right sides of fabric pieces together and use 1/4-inch seam allowances throughout unless otherwise specified.

❖ It is very important that accurate 1/4-inch seam allowances are used. It is wise to stitch a sample 1/4-inch seam allowance to check your machine's seam allowance accuracy.

❖ Press seam allowances in one direction toward the darker fabric and/or in the direction that will create the least bulk.

Hints & Helps for Sewing With Flannel

❖ Because flannel stretches more than other cotton calicos, and because the nap makes them thicker, the quilt design should be simple. Let the fabric and color make the design statement.

❖ Press gently to prevent stretching pieces out of shape.

❖ If you notice a piece of flannel is stretching more than the others, place it on the bottom when stitching on the machine. The natural action of the feed dogs will help prevent it from stretching. You may also find using a walking foot helpful.

❖ Before stitching pieces, strips, or borders together, pin often to prevent fabric from stretching and moving. When stitching longer pieces together, divide the pieces into quarters and pin. Divide into even smaller sections to get more control.

TIP . . . .

Fabric Grain - The lengthwise grain has very little give. Crosswise grain does have a bit more give. When sewing a lengthwise grain edge to a crosswise grain edge, always position the crosswise grain fabric under the lengthwise grain fabric. This will help stabilize the two fabrics and prevent puckering. The 10-1/2-inch edge of the **RED** rectangle is the lengthwise grain and the **GREEN SOLID** strip is the crosswise grain.

QUILT TOP

Note: The yardage given allows for the border strips to be cut on the crosswise grain. Diagonally piece the strips as needed, referring to **Diagonal Piecing** instructions.

Cutting

From **RED PRINT**:
- Cut 1, 10-1/2 x 26-1/2-inch center rectangle
- Cut 3, 4-1/2 x 42-inch strips. From these strips cut:
    2, 4-1/2 x 38-1/2-inch strips
    2, 4-1/2 x 14-1/2-inch strips
- Cut 7 more 4-1/2 x 42-inch strips. From these strips cut:
    2, 4-1/2 x 70-1/2-inch strips
    2, 4-1/2 x 46-1/2-inch strips
- Cut 5, 2-1/2 x 42-inch strips. From these strips cut:
    2, 2-1/2 x 58-1/2-inch strips
    2, 2-1/2 x 38-1/2-inch strips

From **GREEN SOLID**:
- Cut 3, 2-1/2 x 42-inch strips. From these strips cut:
    2, 2-1/2 x 30-1/2-inch strips
    2, 2-1/2 x 10-1/2-inch strips
- Cut 6 more 2-1/2 x 42-inch strips. From these strips cut:
    2, 2-1/2 x 62-1/2-inch strips
    2, 2-1/2 x 42-1/2-inch strips

From **BEIGE PRINT**:
- Cut 4, 4-1/2 x 42-inch strips. From these strips cut:
    2, 4-1/2 x 46-1/2-inch strips
    2, 4-1/2 x 22-1/2-inch strips

From **GREEN PRINT**:
- Cut 5, 4-1/2 x 42-inch strips. From these strips cut:
    2, 4-1/2 x 54-1/2-inch strips
    2, 4-1/2 x 30-1/2-inch strips

Quilt Top Assembly

Step 1
Sew the 2-1/2 x 10-1/2-inch **GREEN SOLID** strips to the top and bottom of the 10-1/2 x 26-1/2-inch **RED** rectangle and press. Sew the 2-1/2 x 30-1/2-inch **GREEN SOLID** strips to the sides of the rectangle and press.

Step 2
Sew the 4-1/2 x 14-1/2-inch **RED** strips to the top and bottom of the quilt top and press. Sew the 4-1/2 x 38-1/2-inch **RED** strips to the sides of the quilt top and press.

Diagonal Piecing

❖ For borders that are longer than 42-inches, piece the border strips together with diagonal seams. They are less visible in a finished quilt than straight seams.

❖ To sew two border strips together diagonally, place them together at a 90° angle with right sides together, as shown below.

Begin stitching here

End stitching here

Each strip should extend approximately 1/4-inch beyond the other. Draw a diagonal line to use as your stitching guide. Sew the two strips together, taking care to start and stop your stitching precisely at the point where the two strips meet, as shown above. Trim away the excess fabric, leaving a 1/4-inch seam allowance, and press the seam open.

❖ Cut enough border strips so that after your strips are stitched together, the diagonal seams will not be at the corners of the quilt top.

Step 3

Sew the 4-1/2 x 22-1/2-inch **BEIGE** strips to the top and bottom of the quilt center and press. Sew the 4-1/2 x 46-1/2-inch **BEIGE** strips to the sides of the quilt top and press.

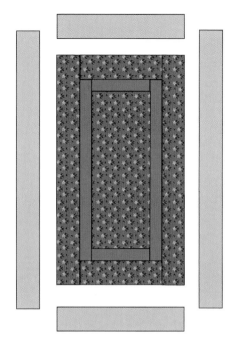

Quilt Assembly Diagram

Step 4

Sew the 4-1/2 x 30-1/2-inch **GREEN PRINT** strips to the top and bottom of the quilt top and press. Sew the 4-1/2 x 54-1/2-inch **GREEN PRINT** strips to the sides of the quilt top and press.

Step 5

Sew the 2-1/2 x 38-1/2-inch **RED** strips to the top and bottom of the quilt top and press. Sew the 2-1/2 x 58-1/2-inch **RED** strips to the sides of the quilt top and press.

Step 6

Sew the 2-1/2 x 42-1/2-inch **GREEN SOLID** strips to the top and bottom of the quilt top and press. Sew the 2-1/2 x 62-1/2-inch **GREEN SOLID** strips to the sides of the quilt top and press.

Step 7

Sew the 4-1/2 x 46-1/2-inch **RED** strips to the top and bottom of the quilt top and press. Sew the 4-1/2 x 70-1/2-inch **RED** strips to the sides of the quilt top and press.

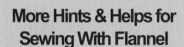

More Hints & Helps for Sewing With Flannel

❖ Consider combining regular cotton calicos with flannels. The different textures complements each other nicely. Using a cotton calico for the backing is another alterntive.

❖ Use a lightweight polyester batting to prevent the quilt from becoming too heavy.

Quilt Assembly Diagram

PUTTING IT ALL TOGETHER

Cut the 3-1/3 yard length of backing fabric in half crosswise to make 2, 1-2/3 yard lengths. Read through **Finishing the Quilt** on page 118 for complete instructions.

BINDING

Cutting

From **RED PLAID**:
Cut enough 6-1/2-inch wide **bias** strips to make a 270-inch long strip

Diagonally piece the strips as needed. Sew the binding to the quilt using a scant 1-inch seam allowance. This measurement will produce a 1-inch wide finished double binding. Read through **Binding** instructions on page 119 for complete instructions.

This quilt is not photographed but included as a great project for leftover fabrics.

HOPSCOTCH

Yardage is based on 42-inch wide fabric.

FABRICS AND SUPPLIES

1	yard	**BLUE PRINT** for quilt top
1	yard	**BLUE/RED/BEIGE PLAID** for quilt top
1	yard	**RED/GREEN CHECK** for quilt top
1	yard	**LIGHT RED PRINT** for quilt top
1	yard	**BLUE/BEIGE CHECK** for quilt top
1-5/8	yards	**RED PRINT** for binding
4	yards	Backing fabric

Quilt batting, at least 70 x 81-inches

A rotary cutter, mat, and wide clear plastic ruler with 1/8-inch markings are needed tools in attaining accuracy. A 6 x 24-inch ruler is recommended.

QUILT TOP

Cutting

From **each** of the 1 yard prints:
- Cut 5, 6 x 42-inch strips. From these strips cut:
     5, 6 x 8-inch rectangles
     5, 6 x 12-inch rectangles
     5, 6 x 20-inch rectangles

Piecing

Step 1

Randomly piece the rectangles into vertical rows taking care to piece each row using sizes indicated in diagram. Sew 3 rows together forming one segment. Make 4 segments. Sew the segments together to make the quilt top.

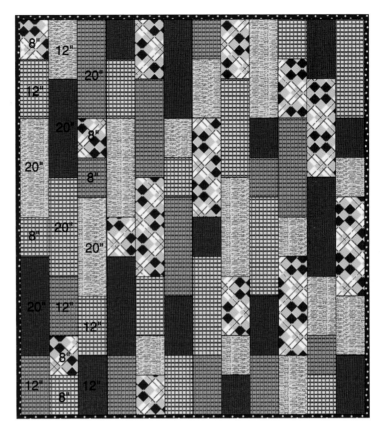

66 x 77-inches

Step 2

When the quilt top is complete, staystitch 1/4-inch around quilt top. This prevents seams from opening up while quilting and binding.

PUTTING IT ALL TOGETHER

Cut the 4 yard length of backing fabric in half crosswise to make 2, 2 yard lengths. Refer to **Finishing the Quilt** on page 118 for complete instructions.

BINDING

Cutting

From binding fabric:
- Cut 8, 6-1/2 x 42-inch strips

Sew the binding to the quilt using a 1-inch seam allowance. This measurement will produce a 1-inch wide finished double binding. Refer to page 119 for **Binding** and **Diagonal Piecing** instructions.

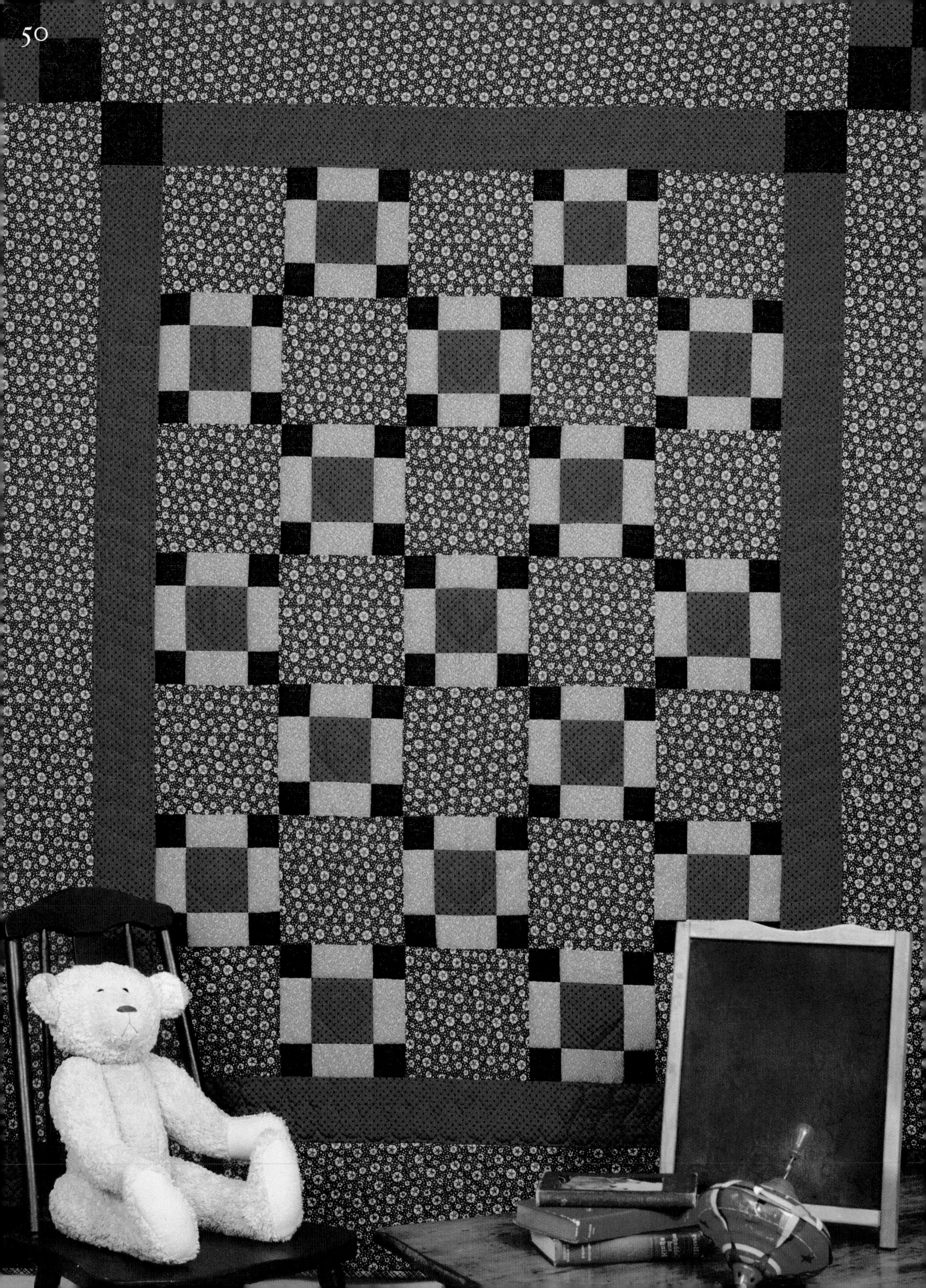

LITTLE BOY BLUE

Yardage is based on 42-inch wide fabric.

FABRICS AND SUPPLIES

3/4	yard	**GOLD PRINT** for pieced blocks
3/4	yard	**BROWN PRINT** for pieced blocks and corner squares
1-1/8	yards	**RED PRINT** for pieced blocks, inner border, and corner squares
3	yards	**BLUE PRINT** for alternate blocks and outer border
3/4	yard	**RED PLAID** for binding (cut on the bias)
4-2/3	yards	Backing fabric

Quilt batting, at least 68 x 84-inches

A rotary cutter, mat, and wide clear plastic ruler with 1/8-inch markings are needed tools in attaining accuracy. A 6 x 24-inch ruler and 12-1/2-inch acrylic square are recommended.

*This is the best kid quilt ever.
It is so easy to make and looks great
in so many color combinations.
Quick easy quilts get used! You know
you can always make another one if
the first wears out. Try this one in
flannel, you will love it.*

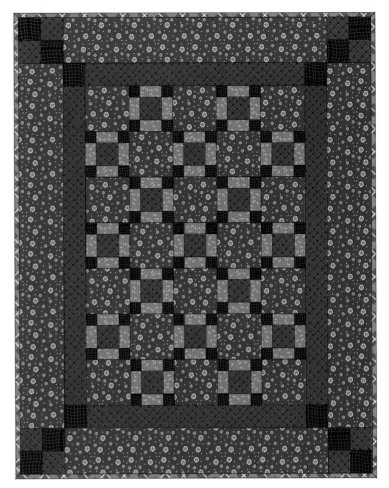

64 x 80-inches
Block: 8-inches square

GETTING STARTED

❖ Read instructions thoroughly before beginning project.

❖ Prewash and press fabrics to test for color fastness and possible shrinkage.

❖ For piecing, place right sides of fabric pieces together and use 1/4-inch seam allowances throughout unless otherwise specified.

❖ It is very important that accurate 1/4-inch seam allowances are used. It is wise to stitch a sample 1/4-inch seam allowance to check your machine's seam allowance accuracy.

❖ Press seam allowances in one direction toward the darker fabric and/or in the direction that will create the least bulk.

❖ Instructions are given for quick cutting and piecing of blocks. Note that for some of the pieces, the quick-cutting method will result in leftover fabric.

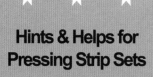

Hints & Helps for Pressing Strip Sets

When sewing strips of fabric together for strip sets, it is important to press the seam allowances nice and flat, usually to the dark fabric. Be careful not to stretch as you press, causing a "rainbow effect." This will affect the accuracy and shape of the pieces cut from the strip set. Press on the wrong side first with the strips perpendicular to the ironing board. Flip the piece over and press on the right side to prevent little pleats from forming at the seams. Laying the strip set lengthwise on the ironing board seems to encourage the rainbow effect, as shown in diagram.

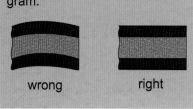

wrong   right

TIP . . . .

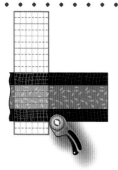

Make a habit of stopping often to check that your ruler is perpendicular to the strip set as you cross-cut your segments. Lining up a horizontal marking on your ruler with a strip set seam will help keep your 2-1/2-inch segments "square."

PIECED BLOCKS & QUILT CENTER

MAKE 17 BLOCKS

Cutting

From **GOLD PRINT**:
- Cut 3, 4-1/2 x 42-inch strips
- Cut 4, 2-1/2 x 42-inch strips

From **BROWN PRINT**:
- Cut 6, 2-1/2 x 42-inch strips

From **RED PRINT**:
- Cut 2, 4-1/2 x 42-inch strips

From **BLUE PRINT**:
- Cut 5, 8-1/2 x 42-inch strips. From these strips cut:
  18, 8-1/2-inch squares for alternate blocks

Piecing

Note: The pieced blocks are made up of strip sets to minimize cutting and piecing. The strips are sewn together, then cut into segments. The segments are then sewn together to form the pieced blocks.

Step 1

Aligning long edges, sew 2-1/2 x 42-inch **BROWN** strips to both sides of a 4-1/2 x 42-inch **GOLD** strip and press toward the **BROWN** strips. Make a total of 3 strip sets. Cut the strip sets into segments.

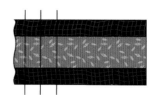

Cut 34, 2-1/2-inch wide segments

Step 2

Aligning long edges, sew 2-1/2 x 42-inch **GOLD** strips to both sides of a 4-1/2 x 42-inch **RED** strip and press toward the **RED** strip. Make a total of 2 strip sets. Cut the strip sets into segments.

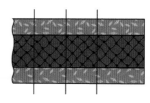

Cut 17, 4-1/2-inch wide segments

Step 3

Sew a Step 1 segment to both sides of a Step 2 segment and press toward the center unit. <u>At this point each pieced block should measure 8-1/2-inches square.</u>

Make 17

Step 4

Referring to the quilt diagram for block placement, sew the pieced blocks and alternate blocks together in 7 rows of 5 blocks each. Press the seam allowances toward the alternate blocks so they will fit snugly together with less bulk.

Step 5

Pin the rows together at the block intersections, and sew the rows together. Press the row seams in one direction.

BORDERS

Note: The yardage given allows for the border strips to be cut on the crosswise grain. Diagonally piece the strips as needed, referring to **Diagonal Piecing** *instructions.*

Cutting

From **RED PRINT**:
- Cut 5, 4-1/2 x 42-inch inner border strips
- Cut 1 more 4-1/2 x 42-inch strip

From **BLUE PRINT**:
- Cut 7, 8-1/2 x 42-inch outer border strips

From **BROWN PRINT**:
- Cut 1, 4-1/2 x 42-inch strip. From this strip cut:
    4, 4-1/2-inch corner squares
- Cut 1 more 4-1/2 x 42-inch strip

Assembling and Attaching the Borders

Step 1

Measure the quilt top from left to right through the middle. Measure and mark the border lengths and center points on the 4-1/2-inch wide **RED** strips. Pin the border strips to the quilt top matching ends and center points, stitch, and press outward. Trim away the excess fabric.

Step 2

For the side borders, measure the quilt top including the seam allowances, but not the top and bottom borders. Cut the **RED** side borders to this length. Sew a 4-1/2-inch **BROWN** corner square to each end of these border strips and press toward **RED** fabric. Sew the borders to the quilt center and press outward.

Step 3

Aligning long edges, sew the 4-1/2-inch wide **RED** and **BROWN** strips together and press. Cut the strip set into segments.

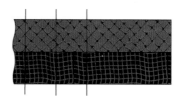

Crosscut 8, 4-1/2-inch
wide segments

Step 4

Sew the Step 3 segments together in pairs and press. <u>At this point the corner squares should measure 8-1/2-inches square.</u>

Make 4

Step 5 To attach the 8-1/2-inch wide **BLUE PRINT** outer border strips with 8-1/2-inch pieced corner squares, refer to Steps 1 and 2.

Border Assembly Diagram

Cutting Bias Binding

❖ To cut bias binding strips, fold the binding yardage on the diagonal, forming a triangle. Using a rotary cutter, mat, and wide acrylic ruler, measure 1/2-inch from the fold, and cut away the folded edge to get a cut straight edge. Move the ruler across the fabric, cutting parallel strips in the desired binding width.

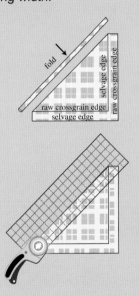

❖ Diagonally piece the bias binding strips together, using as many long strips as possible, with shorter strips placed between the longer strips. Be careful not to stretch the seams as you stitch binding strips together.

PUTTING IT ALL TOGETHER

Cut the 4-2/3 yard length of backing fabric in half crosswise to make 2, 2-1/3 yard lengths. Read through **Finishing the Quilt** on page 118 for complete instructions.

BINDING

Cutting

From **RED PLAID**:
• Cut enough 2-3/4-inch wide **bias** strips to make a 300-inch long strip.

Diagonally piece the binding strips. Sew the binding to the quilt using a 3/8-inch seam allowance. This measurement will produce a 1/2-inch wide finished double binding. Read through **Binding** instructions on page 119 for complete instructions.

PADDLEWHEEL SAWTOOTH TABLE RUNNER

Yardage is based on 42-inch wide fabric.

FABRICS AND SUPPLIES

1/2	yard	**BLUE PRINT** for paddlewheels
1/2	yard	**BEIGE PRINT** for background
1/3	yard	**RED PRINT** for sawtooth border

5 x 42-inch strip **GOLD PRINT** for corner squares

1/2	yard	**RED GRID** for outer border
3/8	yard	**DARK BLUE PRINT** for binding
3/4	yard	Backing fabric

Quilt batting, at least 26 x 44-inches

A rotary cutter, mat, and wide clear plastic ruler with 1/8-inch markings are needed tools in attaining accuracy. A 6 x 24-inch ruler and 12-1/2-inch acrylic square are recommended.

22 x 40-inches
Block: 9-inches square

GETTING STARTED

❖ Read instructions thoroughly before beginning project.

❖ Prewash and press fabrics to test for color fastness and possible shrinkage.

❖ For piecing, place right sides of fabric pieces together and use 1/4-inch seam allowances throughout unless otherwise specified.

❖ It is very important that accurate 1/4-inch seam allowances are used. It is wise to stitch a sample 1/4-inch seam allowance to check your machine's seam allowance accuracy.

❖ Press seam allowances in one direction toward the darker fabric and/or in the direction that will create the least bulk.

❖ Instructions are given for quick cutting and piecing of blocks. Note that for some of the pieces, the quick-cutting method will result in leftover fabric.

PADDLEWHEEL BLOCKS

Make 3 blocks

Cutting

From **BLUE PRINT**:
- Cut 3, 4-1/2-inch squares
- Cut 1, 3-3/8 x 42-inch strip
- Cut 2, 3 x 42-inch strips. From these strips cut:
    12, 3 x 4-1/2-inch rectangles.

From **BEIGE PRINT**:
- Cut 1, 3-3/8 x 42-inch strip
- Cut 1, 3 x 42-inch strip. From this strip cut:
    12, 3-inch squares.

Piecing

Step 1

With right sides together, layer the 3-3/8 x 42-inch **BLUE** and **BEIGE** strips. Press together, but do not sew. Cut the layered strip into squares. Cut the layered squares in half diagonally to make 12 sets of triangles. Stitch a 1/4-inch from the diagonal edge of each pair of triangles and press. <u>At this point each triangle-pieced square should measure 3-inches square</u>.

Crosscut 6, 3-3/8-inch squares

Make 12, 3-inch
triangle-pieced squares

Step 2

Position a 3-inch **BEIGE** square on the left corner of a 3 x 4-1/2-inch **BLUE** rectangle. Draw a diagonal line on the square and stitch on the line. Trim the seam allowance to 1/4-inch, and press.

Make 12

Step 3

Referring to the block diagram, sew a Step 2 unit to the top and bottom edges of a 4-1/2-inch **BLUE** square and press. Make 3 units. Sew Step 1 triangle-pieced squares to both ends of the remaining Step 2 units and press. Sew these units to the side edges of the **BLUE** square and press. <u>At this point each paddlewheel block should measure 9-1/2-inches square</u>.

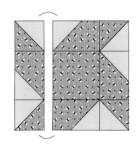

Block Diagram
Make 3

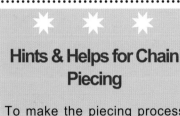

Hints & Helps for Chain Piecing

To make the piecing process for "Paddlewheel Sawtooth Table Runner" more efficient, plan on chain piecing all of the triangle pieced squares at one time.

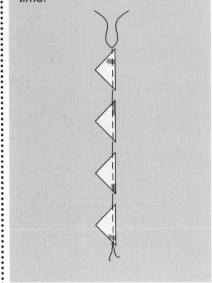

Step 4

Sew the 3 paddlewheel blocks together and press. <u>At this point the runner center should measure 9-1/2 x 27-1/2-inches</u>.

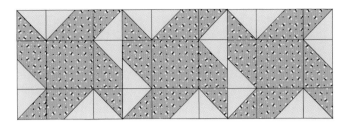

BORDERS

Note: *The yardage given allows for the border strips to be cut on the crosswise grain. Read through **Border** instructions on page 118 for general instructions on adding borders.*

Cutting

From **RED PRINT** :
• Cut 2, 3-7/8 x 42-inch strips

From **BEIGE PRINT**:
• Cut 2, 3-7/8 x 42-inch strips

From **GOLD PRINT**:
• Cut 4, 4-inch corner squares
• Cut 4, 3-1/2-inch corner squares

From **RED GRID**:
• Cut 3, 4 x 42-inch outer border strips

Assembling and Attaching the Borders

Step 1

With right sides together, layer the 3-7/8 x 42-inch **RED PRINT** and **BEIGE** strips together in pairs. Press together, but do not sew. Cut the layered strips into squares. Cut the layered squares in half diagonally to make 24 sets of triangles. Stitch a 1/4-inch from the diagonal edge of each pair of triangles and press. <u>At this point each triangle-pieced square should measure 3-1/2-inches square</u>.

Crosscut 12, 3-7/8-inch squares

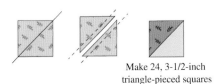

Make 24, 3-1/2-inch
triangle-pieced squares

Borders With Corner Squares

For the side borders, measure the runner top including the seam allowances, but not the top and bottom borders. Cut the 4-inch wide **RED GRID** side borders to this length. Sew a 4-inch **GOLD** corner square to each end of these border strips and press toward the **RED GRID** fabric. Sew the borders to the runner center and press outward.

TIP . . . .

If your sawtooth border does not measure 9-1/2-inches long, make very small adjustments on many seams. The small amounts will be less noticeable than making a large adjustment on one seam.

Step 2

For each 9-1/2-inch edge of the runner, sew together 3 of the Step 1 triangle-pieced squares and press. Sew the sawtooth borders to the runner and press.

Step 3

For each 27-1/2-inch edge of the runner, sew together 9 of the Step 1 triangle-pieced squares and press. Add 3-1/2-inch **GOLD** corner squares to both ends of the sawtooth borders and press. Sew the sawtooth borders to the runner and press.

Step 4

Attach the 4-inch wide **RED GRID** top and bottom outer border strips.

Step 5

Attach the 4-inch wide **RED GRID** side outer border strips with 4-inch **GOLD** corner squares, refer to **Borders with Corner Squares**.

PUTTING IT ALL TOGETHER

Trim the backing and batting so they are 4-inches larger than the runner top. Refer to **Finishing the Quilt** on page 118 for complete instructions.

BINDING

Cutting

From **DARK BLUE PRINT**:
• Cut 4, 2-3/4 x 42-inch strips.

Sew the binding to the quilt using a 3/8-inch seam allowance. This measurement will produce a 1/2-inch wide finished double binding. Refer to page 119 for **Binding** and **Diagonal Piecing** instructions.

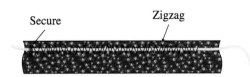

Secure   Zigzag

PILLOW SHAM

20 x 29-inches without ruffle

Yardage is based on 42-inch wide fabric.

FABRICS AND SUPPLIES

1	yard	for pillow front
1-1/8	yards	for pillow ruffle
1-1/8	yards	for pillow back

Quilting thread for gathering ruffle

Queen bed pillow form (20 x 29-inches)

A rotary cutter, mat, and wide clear plastic ruler
with 1/8-inch markings are needed tools in attaining

*Ruffled pillow shams made of coordinating or
matching fabric found in a quilt can quickly turn
a bed quilt into a bed ensemble*

Cutting

From pillow fabric:
- Cut 1, 21 x 30-inch pillow top rectangle
- Cut 2, 21 x 36-inch pillow back rectangles
- Cut 6, 6-1/2 x 42-inch ruffle strips

Attach the Ruffle

Step 1
Diagonally piece together the 6-1/2-inch wide ruffle strips
to make a continuous ruffle strip, referring to **Diagonal
Piecing** on page 68.

Step 2
Fold the strip in half lengthwise, wrong sides together,
and press. Divide the ruffle strip into 4 equal segments,
and mark the quarter points with safety pins.

Step 3
To gather the ruffle, position quilting thread (or pearl cotton)
1/4-inch from the raw edges of the folded ruffle strip.
You will need a length of thread 200-inches long. Secure
one end of the thread by stitching across it. Zigzag stitch
over the thread all the way around the ruffle strip, taking
care not to sew through it.

Step 4
Divide the edges of the 21 x 30-inch pillow front rectangle into 4 equal segments and mark the quarter
points with safety pins. With right sides together and
raw edges aligned, pin the ruffle to the pillow top,
matching the quarter points. Pull up the gathering
stitches until the ruffle fits the pillow front, taking
care to allow extra fullness in the ruffle at each corner. Sew the ruffle to the pillow front, using a 1/4-
inch seam allowance. See page 80 for illustration of
attaching ruffle.

Assembling the Pillow Back

Step 1
With wrong sides together, fold each 21 x
36-inch pillow back rectangle in half crosswise to
form 2, 18 x 21-inch double-thick pillow back pieces.
Overlap the 2 folded edges so the pillow back measures 21 x 30-inches. Pin the pieces together and
stitch around the entire piece to create a single pillow
back, using a scant 1/4-inch seam allowance.

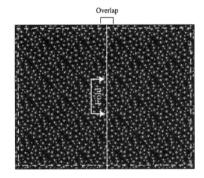

Overlap

Step 2
With right sides together, layer the pillow back and
the pillow front, and pin. The ruffle will be sandwiched between the 2 layers and turned toward the
center of the pillow at this time. Pin and stitch
around the outside edges using a 1/2-inch seam
allowance.

Step 3
Turn the pillow sham right side out, insert the pillow
form through the pillow back opening, and fluff up
the ruffle.

PINE STAR RUNNER

Yardage is based on 42-inch wide fabric.

FABRICS AND SUPPLIES

1/4	yard	**GREEN PRINT #1** for tree points
1/2	yard	**BEIGE PRINT** for background
5/8	yard	**GREEN PRINT #2** for trees and border
1/8	yard	**BLACK PRINT** for tree trunk units
3/4	yard	**RED PRINT #1** for star, and side and corner triangles
1/2	yard	**RED PRINT #2** for binding
1-1/2	yards	Backing fabric

Quilt batting, at least 27 x 61-inches

A rotary cutter, mat, and wide clear plastic ruler with 1/8-inch markings are needed tools in attaining accuracy. A 6 x 24-inch ruler and 12-1/2-inch acrylic square are recommended.

Pine Star Runner showcases two very visually strong blocks in deep rich colors set against a cream background for high contrast. This runner would certainly dress up any table for the holidays. If you have a long table, make three runners and place the runners crosswise creating six placemats.

23 x 57-inches
Block: 12-inches square

GETTING STARTED

❖ Read instructions thoroughly before beginning project.

❖ Prewash and press fabrics to test for color fastness and possible shrinkage.

❖ For piecing, place right sides of fabric pieces together and use 1/4-inch seam allowances throughout unless otherwise specified.

❖ It is very important that accurate 1/4-inch seam allowances are used. It is wise to stitch a sample 1/4-inch seam allowance to check your machine's seam allowance accuracy.

❖ Press seam allowances in one direction toward the darker fabric and/or in the direction that will create the least bulk.

❖ Instructions are given for quick cutting and piecing of blocks. Note that for some of the pieces, the quick-cutting method will result in leftover fabric.

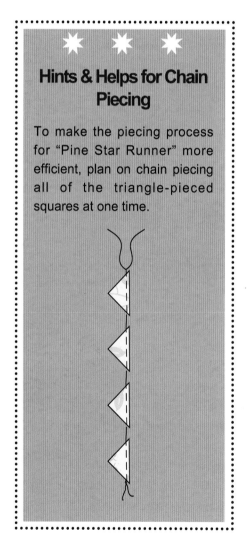

Hints & Helps for Chain Piecing

To make the piecing process for "Pine Star Runner" more efficient, plan on chain piecing all of the triangle-pieced squares at one time.

TREE BLOCKS

MAKE 2 BLOCKS

Cutting

From **GREEN PRINT #1**:
- Cut 1, 2-7/8 x 42-inch strip
- Cut 2, 2-1/2-inch squares

From **BEIGE PRINT**:
- Cut 2, 6-inch squares
- Cut 1, 2-7/8 x 42-inch strip
- Cut 4, 2-1/2-inch squares

From **GREEN PRINT #2**:
- Cut 1, 4-1/2 x 42-inch strip. From this strip cut:
     2, 4-1/2 x 8-1/2-inch rectangles
     2, 4-1/2-inch squares

From **BLACK PRINT**:
- Cut 2, 1-3/4 x 11-inch strips

Piecing

Step 1

With right sides together, layer the 2-7/8 x 42-inch **GREEN #1** and **BEIGE** strips. Press together, but do not sew. Cut the layered strip into squares. Cut the layered squares in half diagonally to make 24 sets of triangles. Stitch 1/4-inch from the diagonal edge of each pair of triangles and press toward the **GREEN** triangle. <u>At this point each triangle-pieced square should measure 2-1/2-inches square</u>.

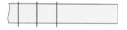

Crosscut 12, 2-7/8-inch squares

Make 24, 2-1/2-inch triangle-pieced squares

Step 2

Sew the triangle-pieced squares together in pairs and press. Refer to the diagram for color placement.

 Make 6 Unit A

 Make 6 Unit B

Step 3

Sew a Unit A to both ends of a 4-1/2 x 8-1/2-inch **GREEN PRINT #2** rectangle and press toward the rectangle. <u>At this point each unit should measure 4-1/2 x 12-1/2-inches</u>.

Make 2

Step 4

Sew a Unit A to the left side of a 4-1/2-inch **GREEN #2** square and press toward Unit A.

Make 2

Step 5

Sew a 2-1/2-inch **BEIGE** square to the left side of a Unit B, and press toward the unit. Sew this unit to the bottom of a Step 4 unit and press toward the Step 4 unit. <u>At this point each unit should measure 6-1/2-inches square</u>.

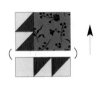

Make 2

Step 6

Sew the remaining B Units together in pairs and press. Sew a 2-1/2-inch **GREEN #1** square to the left side of each unit and press toward the **GREEN** square. Sew a 2-1/2-inch **BEIGE** square to the right side of each unit and press toward the **BEIGE** square. Sew these units to the top of the Step 3 units and press. <u>At this point each unit should measure 6-1/2 x 12-1/2-inches</u>.

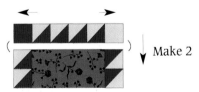

Make 2

TIP . . . .

A 12-1/2-inch square acrylic ruler is great for squaring up individual blocks and corners of a quilt top, for cutting strips up to 12-1/2-inches wide or long, and for trimming side and corner triangles.

Step 7

Cut the 6-inch **BEIGE** squares in half diagonally. Center a **BEIGE** triangle on a 1-3/4 x 11-inch **BLACK** strip. Stitch a 1/4-inch seam and press the seam allowance toward the **BLACK** strip. Center another **BEIGE** triangle on the **BLACK** strip, stitch and press toward the **BLACK** strip. The trunk strip will extend beyond the triangles. Use your clear acrylic ruler to trim and square this unit to 6-1/2-inches square.

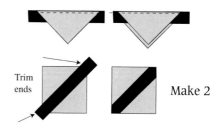

Make 2

Step 8

Sew the trunk units to the right side of the Step 5 units and press toward the Step 5 unit.

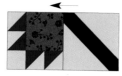

Make 2

Step 9

Sew the Step 8 units to the bottom of the Step 6 units and press. <u>At this point each block should measure 12-1/2-inches square</u>.

Make 2

STAR BLOCK

MAKE 1 BLOCK

Cutting

From **RED PRINT**:
- Cut 1, 4-1/2-inch square
- Cut 8, 2-1/2-inch squares

From **BEIGE PRINT**:
- Cut 2, 2-1/2 x 42-inch strips. From these strips cut:
  - 2, 2-1/2 x 12-1/2-inch rectangles
  - 2, 2-1/2 x 8-1/2-inch rectangles
  - 4, 2-1/2 x 4-1/2-inch rectangles
  - 4, 2-1/2-inch squares

Piecing

Step 1

Position a 2-1/2-inch **RED** square on the left side of a 2-1/2 x 4-1/2-inch **BEIGE** rectangle. Draw a diagonal line on the square, stitch, trim, and press toward the dark triangle. Repeat this process at the opposite side of the rectangle.

   　　Make 4

Step 2

Sew Step 1 units to the top and bottom of the 4-1/2-inch **RED** square and press toward the center square. Sew 2-1/2-inch **BEIGE** squares to both sides of the remaining Step 1 units and press toward the **BEIGE** squares. Sew these units to the sides of the star and press toward the center. At this point the star should measure 8-1/2-inches square.

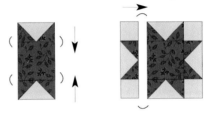

Step 3

Sew 2-1/2 x 8-1/2-inch **BEIGE** rectangles to the top and bottom of the star block and press outward. Sew 2-1/2 x 12-1/2-inch **BEIGE** rectangles to the sides of the star block and press outward. At this point the star block should measure 12-1/2-inches square.

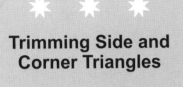

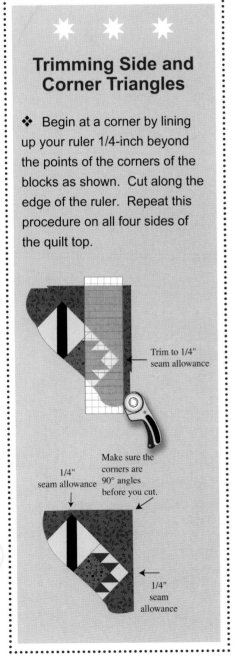

Trimming Side and Corner Triangles

❖ Begin at a corner by lining up your ruler 1/4-inch beyond the points of the corners of the blocks as shown. Cut along the edge of the ruler. Repeat this procedure on all four sides of the quilt top.

Trim to 1/4" seam allowance

1/4" seam allowance

Make sure the corners are 90° angles before you cut.

1/4" seam allowance

RUNNER CENTER

Cutting

From **RED PRINT #1**:

- Cut 1, 19 x 42-inch strip. From this strip cut:

    1, 19-inch square, cutting it twice diagonally to make 4 side triangles.

Diagonal Piecing

❖ For borders that are longer than 42-inches, piece the border strips together with diagonal seams. They are less visible in a finished quilt than straight seams.

❖ To sew two border strips together diagonally, place them together at a 90° angle with right sides together, as shown below.

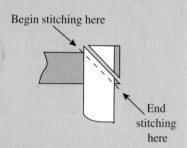

Begin stitching here

End stitching here

Each strip should extend approximately 1/4-inch beyond the other. Draw a diagonal line to use as your stitching guide. Sew the two strips together, taking care to start and stop your stitching precisely at the point where the two strips meet, as shown above. Trim away the excess fabric, leaving a 1/4-inch seam allowance, and press the seam open.

❖ Cut enough border strips, so after your strips are stitched together, the diagonal seams will not be at the corners of the quilt top.

19-inch square

side triangles

10-inch square

corner triangles

Also cut 2, 10-inch squares, cutting each square once diagonally to make 4 corner triangles.

Note: The side and corner triangles are larger than needed and will be trimmed later.

Runner Center Assembly

Step 1

Referring to the border assembly diagram, sew the tree blocks, star block, and side triangles together in 3 diagonal rows. Press the seam allowances toward the side triangles so seams will fit snugly together with less bulk.

Step 2

Pin the rows at the block intersections and sew the rows together. Press the row seams in one direction.

Step 3

Sew the corner triangles to the runner and press.

Step 4

Trim away the excess fabric from the side and corner triangles, taking care to allow a 1/4-inch seam allowance beyond the corners of each block. Refer to **Trimming Side and Corner Triangles** on page 67 for complete instructions.

BORDER

Note: The yardage given allows for the border strips to be cut on the crosswise grain. Diagonally piece the strips as needed, referring to **Diagonal Piecing** instructions. Read through **Border** instructions on page 118 for general instructions on adding borders.

Cutting

From **GREEN PRINT #2**:
• Cut 4, 3-1/2 x 42-inch border strips

QUILTING DESIGNS . . . .

Quilting suggestions
for runner

When using a purchased quilting
stencil it is sometimes necessary
to shift the template and make
small adjustments to make the
design fit your border. Test your
design on a length of freezer paper
cut to the size of your borders to
determine where adjustments
should be made.

Attaching the Border

Attach the 3-1/2-inch wide
GREEN #2 border strips to
the runner.

PUTTING IT ALL TOGETHER

Cut the 1-1/2 yard length of
backing fabric in half crosswise to make 2, 3/4 yard
lengths. Read through
Finishing the Quilt on page
118 for complete instructions.

BINDING

Cutting

From **RED PRINT #2**:
• Cut 4, 2-3/4 x 42-inch strips

Diagonally piece the strips as needed. Sew the binding to the runner using a
3/8-inch seam allowance. This measurement will produce a 1/2-inch wide
finished double binding. Read through **Binding** instructions on page 119 for
complete instructions.

Border Assembly Diagram

PINWHEEL POINT

Yardage is based on 42-inch wide fabric.

FABRICS AND SUPPLIES

1	yard	**PLUM PRINT** for pinwheel blocks and inner border
1/2	yard	**GOLD PRINT** for pinwheel blocks
1	yard	**BEIGE PRINT** for alternate blocks, and side and corner triangles
1/3	yard	**GREEN PRINT** for middle border
1-2/3	yards	**EGGPLANT PRINT** for outer border
3/4	yard	**PLUM PLAID** for binding (cut on the bias)
3-1/2	yards	Backing fabric

Quilt batting, at least 61 x 72-inches

A rotary cutter, mat, and wide clear plastic ruler with 1/8-inch markings are needed tools in attaining accuracy. A 6 x 24-inch ruler and 12-1/2-inch acrylic square are recommended.

The pinwheel block is one of the oldest traditional quilt blocks. It is always an appropriate choice for many prints whether traditional or contemporary. The alternating block makes this project a fast and easy quilt to piece.

56 x 68-inches
Block: 8-inches square

GETTING STARTED

❖ Read instructions thoroughly before beginning project.

❖ Prewash and press fabrics to test for color fastness and possible shrinkage.

❖ For piecing, place right sides of fabric pieces together and use 1/4-inch seam allowances throughout unless otherwise specified.

❖ It is very important that accurate 1/4-inch seam allowances are used. It is wise to stitch a sample 1/4-inch seam allowance to check your machine's seam allowance accuracy.

❖ Press seam allowances in one direction toward the darker fabric and/or in the direction that will create the least bulk.

❖ Instructions are given for quick cutting and piecing of blocks. Note that for some of the pieces, the quick-cutting method will result in leftover fabric.

TIP . . . .

Pressing the layered strips together before cutting prevents the fabric from shifting and makes it easier to be more accurate.

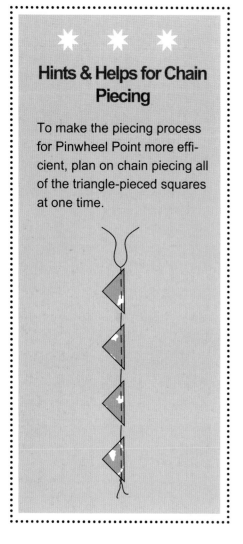

Hints & Helps for Chain Piecing

To make the piecing process for Pinwheel Point more efficient, plan on chain piecing all of the triangle-pieced squares at one time.

TIP . . . .

Check each pinwheel block as you sew them to make sure they match the diagram. This will insure all the pinwheels are going the same direction.

PINWHEEL BLOCKS

MAKE 12 BLOCKS

Cutting

From **PLUM PRINT**:
• Cut 3, 4-7/8 x 42-inch strips

From **GOLD PRINT**:
• Cut 3, 4-7/8 x 42-inch strips

Piecing

Step 1

With right sides together, layer the 4-7/8 x 42-inch **PLUM** and **GOLD** strips in pairs. Press together, but do not sew. Cut the layered strips into squares. Cut the layered squares in half diagonally to make 48 sets of triangles. Stitch 1/4-inch from the diagonal edge of each pair of triangles and press. <u>At this point each triangle-pieced square should measure 4-1/2-inches square</u>.

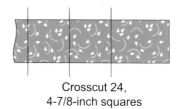

Crosscut 24,
4-7/8-inch squares

Make 48,
4-1/2-inch triangle
pieced squares

Step 2

Referring to the diagram, sew the triangle-pieced squares together in pairs and press. Sew the pairs together to make the pinwheel block. <u>At this point each pinwheel block should measure 8-1/2-inches square.</u>

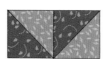

Make 24

Make 12

QUILT CENTER

Cutting

Note: *The side and corner triangles are larger than necessary and will be trimmed before the borders are added.*

From **BEIGE PRINT**:
- Cut 1, 13 x 42-inch strip. From this strip cut:
  3, 13-inch squares, cutting each twice diagonally for a total of 12 triangles.
  You will be using only 10 for side triangles.
- Cut 2, 8-1/2 x 42-inch strips. From these strips cut:
  6, 8-1/2-inch alternate block squares.
  Also, cut 2, 8-inch squares, cutting each once diagonally for a total of 4 corner triangles.

Quilt Center Assembly

Step 1
Referring to the quilt center assembly diagram for block placement, sew together the pinwheel blocks, 8-1/2-inch alternate blocks, and side triangles in 6 diagonal rows. Press the seam allowances toward the alternate blocks and side triangles.

Quilt Center Assembly Diagram

Step 2
Pin the rows together at the block intersections and sew. Press the row seams in one direction.

Trimming Side and Corner Triangles

❖ Begin at a corner by lining up your ruler 1/4-inch beyond the points of the corners of the blocks as shown. Cut along the edge of the ruler. Repeat this procedure on all four sides of the quilt top.

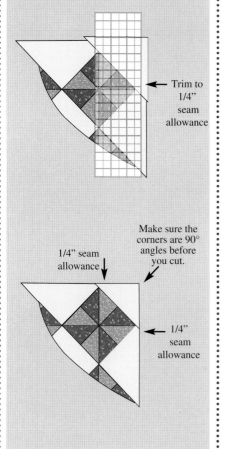

← Trim to 1/4" seam allowance

Make sure the corners are 90° angles before you cut.

1/4" seam allowance

← 1/4" seam allowance

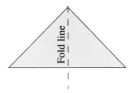

Diagonal Piecing

❖ For borders that are longer than 42-inches, piece the border strips together with diagonal seams. They are less visible in a finished quilt than straight seams.

❖ To sew two border strips together diagonally, place them together at a 90° angle with right sides together, as shown below.

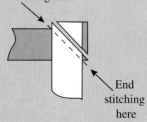

Begin stitching here

End stitching here

Each strip should extend approximately 1/4-inch beyond the other. Draw a diagonal line to use as your stitching guide. Sew the two strips together, taking care to start and stop your stitching precisely at the point where the two strips meet, as shown above. Trim away the excess fabric, leaving a 1/4-inch seam allowance, and press the seam open.

❖ Cut enough border strips so after your strips are stitched together, the diagonal seams will not be at the corners of the quilt top.

Step 3

Sew the corner triangles to the quilt center and press. To determine the center of the corner triangle, fold the triangle in half and finger press the halfway point.

Unfold, and with right sides together pin the center point of the corner triangle edge to match the pinwheel block seam intersection, and stitch.

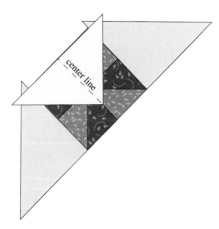

Step 4

Trim away the excess fabric from the side and corner triangles taking care to allow a 1/4-inch seam allowance beyond the corners of each block. Read through **Trimming Side and Corner Triangles** on page 73 for complete instructions.

BORDERS

*Note: The yardage given allows for the border strips to be cut on the crosswise grain. Diagonally piece the strips as needed, referring to **Diagonal Piecing** instructions. Read through **Border** instructions on page 118 for general instructions on adding borders.*

Cutting

From **PLUM PRINT**:
- Cut 5, 2-1/2 x 42-inch inner border strips

From **GREEN PRINT**:
- Cut 5, 1-1/2 x 42-inch middle border strips

From **EGGPLANT PRINT**:
- Cut 6, 9 x 42-inch outer border strips

Attaching the Borders

Step 1
Attach the 2-1/2-inch wide **PLUM** inner border strips.

Step 2
Attach the 1-1/2-inch wide **GREEN** middle border strips.

TIP . . . .

Plaid and checked bindings look best when cut on the bias. Bias plaids add additional interesting design elements to a quilt.

Step 3

Attach the 9-inch wide **EGGPLANT** outer border strips.

Border Assembly Diagram

✻ ✻ ✻
Cutting Bias Binding

❖ To cut bias binding strips, fold the binding yardage on the diagonal, forming a triangle. Using a rotary cutter, mat, and wide acrylic ruler, measure 1/2-inch from the fold, and cut away the folded edge to get a cut straight edge. Move the ruler across the fabric, cutting parallel strips in the desired binding width.

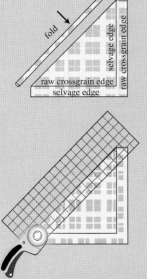

❖ Diagonally piece the bias binding strips together, using as many long strips as possible, with shorter strips placed between the longer strips. Be careful not to stretch the seams as you stitch binding strips together.

PUTTING IT ALL TOGETHER

Cut the 3-1/2 yard length of backing fabric in half crosswise to make 2, 1-3/4 yard lengths. Read through **Finishing the Quilt** on page 118 for complete instructions.

BINDING

Cutting

From **PLUM PLAID**:

• Cut enough 2-3/4-inch wide **bias** strips to make a 260-inch long strip

Diagonally piece the strips as needed. Sew the binding to the quilt using a 3/8-inch seam allowance. This measurement will produce a 1/2-inch wide finished double binding. Read through **Binding** instructions on page 119 for complete instructions.

THREE SEASONS PILLOW

Yardage is based on 42-inch wide fabric.

FABRICS AND SUPPLIES

6 x 26-inch piece **BLUE PRINT** for star

1/8	yard	**GOLD PRINT** for pillow top
3/4	yard	**RED PRINT** for pillow top and ruffle
1/8	yard	**BEIGE PRINT** for pillow top
1/4	yard	**TEAL PRINT** for pillow top
2/3	yard	**RED PRINT** for pillow back

18-inch square of muslin lining for pillow top

Quilt batting, at least 18-inches square

Quilting thread or pearl cotton for gathering ruffle

16-inch pillow form

A rotary cutter, mat, and wide clear plastic ruler with 1/8-inch markings are needed tools in attaining accuracy. A 6 x 24-inch ruler and 12-1/2-inch acrylic square are recommended.

Pillows are an easy decorating makeover for very little money or effort. This pillow made in different color combinations can give a seasonal touch to a room. It would also make a wonderful handmade gift.

16-inches square without ruffle

GETTING STARTED

❖ Read instructions thoroughly before beginning project.

❖ Prewash and press fabrics to test for color fastness and possible shrinkage.

❖ For piecing, place right sides of fabric pieces together and use 1/4-inch seam allowances throughout unless otherwise specified.

❖ It is very important that accurate 1/4-inch seam allowances are used. It is wise to stitch a sample 1/4-inch seam allowance to check your machine's seam allowance accuracy.

❖ Press seam allowances in one direction toward the darker fabric and/or in the direction that will create the least bulk.

PILLOW TOP

Cutting

From **BLUE PRINT**:
- Cut 1, 4-1/2-inch square
- Cut 8, 2-1/2-inch squares

From **GOLD PRINT**:
- Cut 1, 2-1/2 x 42-inch strip. From this strip cut:
    - 4, 2-1/2 x 4-1/2-inch rectangles
    - 8, 2-1/2-inch squares

From **RED PRINT**:
- Cut 1, 2-1/2 x 42-inch strip. From this strip cut:
    - 12, 2-1/2-inch squares

From **BEIGE PRINT**:
- Cut 1, 1-1/2 x 42-inch strip. From this strip cut:
    - 8, 1-1/2 x 2-1/2-inch rectangles

From **TEAL PRINT**:
- Cut 2, 2-1/2 x 16-12-inch border strips
- Cut 2, 2-1/2 x 12-12-inch border strips

Piecing

Step 1
Position a 2-1/2-inch **BLUE** square on the left side of a 2-1/2 x 4-1/2-inch **GOLD** rectangle. Draw a diagonal line on the **BLUE** square and stitch on the line. Trim the seam allowance to 1/4-inch and press toward the dark triangle. Repeat this process at the opposite side of the rectangle.

Make 4

Step 2
Sew Step 1 units to the top and bottom edges of the 4-1/2-inch **BLUE** square and press toward center square. Sew 2-1/2-inch **GOLD** squares to both ends of the remaining Step 1 units and press. Sew these units to both sides of the unit just sewn and press. At this point the star block should measure 8-1/2-inches square.

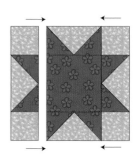

Step 3

Sew together 2 of the 1-1/2 x 2-1/2-inch **BEIGE** rectangles and 3 of the 2-1/2-inch **RED** squares and press toward darker fabric.

Make 4

Step 4

Sew 2 of the Step 3 units to the top and bottom of the star block and press away from the star block. Sew 2-1/2-inch **GOLD** squares to both ends of the remaining Step 3 units and press. Sew these units to both sides of the unit just sewn and press away from the star block. <u>At this point the pillow center should measure 12-1/2-inches square.</u>

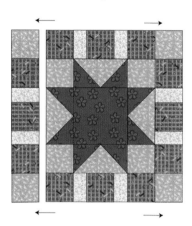

Step 5

Referring to the diagram, sew the 2-1/2 x 12-1/2-inch **TEAL** border strips to the top and bottom of the pillow center and press. Sew the 2-1/2 x 16-1/2-inch **TEAL** border strips to the sides of the pillow center and press. <u>At this point the pillow top should measure 16-1/2-inches square.</u>

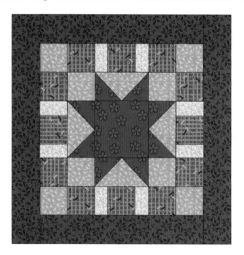

PUTTING IT ALL TOGETHER

Layer the 18-inch muslin lining square, batting, and pillow top. Baste the layers together and quilt as desired.

QUILTING DESIGNS . . . .

Quilting suggestions for pillow top

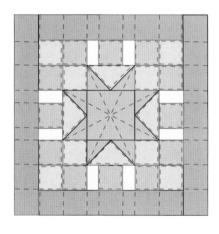

. . . .

TIP . . . .

To prepare the pillow top before attaching the ruffle, hand-baste the edges of the 3 layers together. This will prevent the edges from rippling when you attach the ruffle.

TIP . . . .

This ruffle technique eliminates the need for an extra machine ruffle attachment. It also produces a very nice, full ruffle. The zigzag step eliminates broken gathering stitches and makes it easy to distribute fullness.

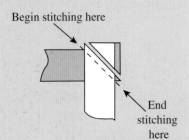

Diagonal Piecing

❖ To sew the ruffle strips together diagonally, place them at a 90° angle with right sides together, as shown below.

Begin stitching here

End stitching here

Each strip should extend approximately 1/4-inch beyond the other. Draw a diagonal line to use as your stitching guide. Sew the two strips together, taking care to start and stop your stitching precisely at the point where the two strips meet, as shown above. Trim away the excess fabric, leaving a 1/4-inch seam allowance, and press the seam open.

PILLOW RUFFLE

Cutting

From **RED PRINT**:
• Cut 5, 4-1/2 x 42-inch strips

Attaching the Ruffle

Step 1
Diagonally piece the ruffle strips together to make a continuous ruffle, referring to **Diagonal Piecing** instructions.

Step 2
Fold the strip in half lengthwise, wrong sides together and press. Divide the ruffle strip into 4 equal parts and mark the quarter points with safety pins.

Step 3
To gather the ruffle, position quilting thread (or pearl cotton) 1/4-inch from the raw edges of the folded ruffle strip. You will need a length of thread 200-inches long. Secure one end of the thread by stitching across it. Zigzag stitch over the thread all the way around the ruffle, taking care not to sew through the thread. This will create a space for the thread to pull through freely, creating the gathers.

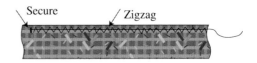

Secure   Zigzag

Step 4
Divide the edges of the pillow top into 4 equal segments and mark the quarter points with safety pins. With right sides together and raw edges aligned, pin the ruffle to the pillow top, matching the quarter points. Pull up the gathering stitches until the ruffle fits the pillow top, pin at close intervals, taking care to allow extra fullness at each corner. Sew the ruffle to the pillow top, using a 1/4-inch seam allowance.

COLOR OPTION 1

COLOR OPTION 2

PILLOW BACK

Cutting

From **RED PRINT**:
• Cut 2, 16-1/2 x 22-inch pillow back rectangles

Assembling the Pillow Back

Step 1

With wrong sides together, fold each 16-1/2 x 22-inch **RED** pillow back rectangle in half crosswise to form 2, 11 x 16-1/2-inch double-thick pillow back pieces. Overlap the 2 folded edges so the pillow back measures 16-1/2-inches square. Pin the pieces together and machine baste around the entire piece to create a single pillow back, using a scant 1/4-inch seam allowance. The double thickness of each back piece will make the pillow back more stable and give it a nice finishing touch.

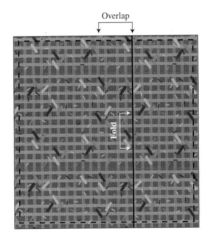

Step 2

With right sides together, layer the pillow back and the pillow top, and pin. The ruffle will be sandwiched between the 2 layers and turned toward the center of the pillow at this time. Pin often and stitch around the outside edges using a 3/8-inch seam allowance.

Step 3

Turn the pillow right side out, insert the pillow form through the pillow back opening, and fluff the ruffle.

TIMBER TREES

Yardage is based on 42-inch wide fabric.

FABRICS AND SUPPLIES

1/8	yard	**GREEN PRINT #1** for tree top unit
1/8	yard	**GREEN PRINT #2** for tree center unit
1/8	yard	**GREEN PRINT #3** for tree bottom unit
5/8	yard	**BEIGE PRINT** for background and checkerboard border
1/8	yard	**BROWN PRINT** for tree trunk unit
1/8	yard	**GOLD PRINT** for inner border
1/4	yard	**RED PRINT** for checkerboard border
1/3	yard	**GREEN PRINT #4** for binding
7/8	yard	Backing fabric

Quilt batting, at least 30-inches square

A rotary cutter, mat, and wide clear plastic ruler with 1/8-inch markings are needed tools in attaining accuracy. A 6 x 24-inch ruler and 12-1/2-inch acrylic square are recommended.

The simplicity of the tree blocks and the checkerboard border create a graphic, striking little wall quilt that also makes a perfect table topper.

26-inches square
Block: 8-inches square

GETTING STARTED

❖ Read instructions thoroughly before beginning project.

❖ Prewash and press fabrics to test for color fastness and possible shrinkage.

❖ For piecing, place right sides of fabric pieces together and use 1/4-inch seam allowances throughout unless otherwise specified.

❖ It is very important that accurate 1/4-inch seam allowances are used. It is wise to stitch a sample 1/4-inch seam allowance to check your machine's seam allowance accuracy.

❖ Press seam allowances in one direction toward the darker fabric and/or in the direction that will create the least bulk.

❖ Instructions are given for quick cutting and piecing of blocks. Note that for some of the pieces, the quick-cutting method will result in leftover fabric.

TREE BLOCKS

MAKE 4 BLOCKS

Cutting

From **GREEN PRINT #1**:
- Cut 4, 2-1/2 x 4-1/2-inch rectangles

From **GREEN PRINT #2**:
- Cut 4, 2-1/2 x 8-1/2-inch rectangles

From **GREEN PRINT #3**:
- Cut 4, 2-1/2 x 8-1/2-inch rectangles

From **BEIGE PRINT**:
- Cut 2, 3-1/2 x 13-inch strips
- Cut 2 , 2-1/2 x 42-inch strips. From these strips cut:
    8, 2-1/2 x 4-1/2-inch rectangles
    16, 2-1/2-inch squares

From **BROWN PRINT**:
- Cut 1, 2-1/2 x 13-inch strip

Piecing

Step 1

Position a 2-1/2 x 4-1/2-inch **BEIGE** rectangle on the left side of a 2-1/2 x 4-1/2-inch **GREEN #1** rectangle. Draw a diagonal line on the **BEIGE** rectangle and stitch on the line. Trim the seam allowance to 1/4-inch and press toward the light fabric. Repeat this process at the opposite side of the **GREEN #1** rectangle. <u>At this point each tree top unit should measure 2-1/2 x 8-1/2-inches.</u>

Make 4
tree top units

Step 2

Position a 2-1/2-inch **BEIGE** square on the left side of a 2-1/2 x 8-1/2-inch **GREEN #2** rectangle. Draw a diagonal line on the square, stitch, trim, and press toward the dark fabric. Repeat this process at the opposite side of the rectangle. <u>At this point each tree center unit should measure 2-1/2 x 8-1/2-inches.</u>

Make 4
tree center units

TIP . . . .

Stitch on the outer edge just a "hair" or a thread width from the marked diagonal line.

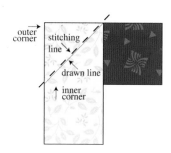

If you stitch on the inner corner side of the diagonal line you will actually make the triangle smaller.

TIP . . . .

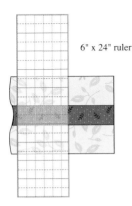

6" x 24" ruler

Make a habit of stopping often to check that your ruler is perpendicular to the strip set as you crosscut your segments. Lining up a horizontal marking on your ruler with a strip set seam will help keep your 2-1/2-inch segments "square."

TIP . . . .

Blocks will fit together more easily and with less bulk if row seams are pressed in opposite directions.

Step 3

Position a 2-1/2-inch **BEIGE** square on the left side of a 2-1/2 x 8-1/2-inch **GREEN #3** rectangle. Draw a diagonal line on the square, stitch, trim, and press toward the dark fabric. Repeat this process at the opposite side of the rectangle. <u>At this point each tree bottom unit should measure 2-1/2 x 8-1/2-inches.</u>

Make 4
tree bottom units

Step 4

To make the tree trunk units, sew a 3-1/2 x 13-inch **BEIGE** strip to both sides of the 2-1/2 x 13-inch **BROWN** strip and press toward the dark fabric. Cut the strip set into segments. <u>At this point each tree trunk unit should measure 2-1/2 x 8-1/2-inches.</u>

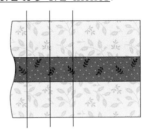

Crosscut 4, 2-1/2-inch
wide segments

Step 5

Referring to the block diagram, sew the Step 1, 2, 3, and 4 units together. Press row seams of 2 tree blocks in one direction, and press row seams of the remaining tree blocks in the opposite direction. <u>At this point each tree block should measure 8-1/2-inches square.</u>

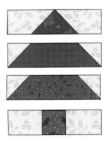
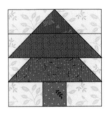

Make 4

Step 6

Referring to the quilt diagram, sew the tree blocks together in pairs and press. Sew the pairs together and press. <u>At this point the quilt center should measure 16-1/2-inches square.</u>

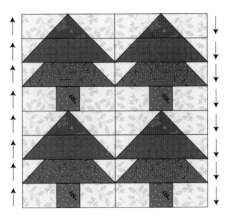

Arrows indicate the direction
the row seams are pressed.

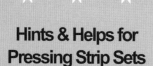

Hints & Helps for Pressing Strip Sets

When sewing strips of fabric together for strip sets, it is important to press the seam allowances nice and flat, usually to the dark fabric. Be careful not to stretch as you press, causing a "rainbow effect." This will affect the accuracy and shape of the pieces cut from the strip set. Press on the wrong side first, with the strips perpendicular to the ironing board. Flip the piece over and press on the right side to prevent little pleats from forming at the seams. Laying the strip set lengthwise on the ironing board seems to encourage the rainbow effect, as shown in diagram.

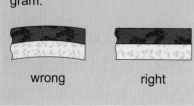

wrong   right

TIP . . . .

If your checkerboard border does not measure 18-1/2-inches long, make very small adjustments on many seams. The small amounts will be less noticeable than making a large adjustment on one seam.

BORDERS

Note: Read through **Border** instructions on page 118 for general instructions on adding borders.

Cutting

From **GOLD PRINT**:
- Cut 2, 1-1/2 x 42-inch inner border strips

From **RED PRINT**:
- Cut 3, 2-1/2 x 42-inch strips for checkerboard border

From **BEIGE PRINT**:
- Cut 3, 2-1/2 x 42-inch strips for checkerboard border

Attaching the Borders

Step 1
Attach the 1-1/2-inch wide **GOLD** inner border strips.

Step 2
Aligning long edges, sew the 2-1/2 x 42-inch **BEIGE** and **RED** strips together in pairs. Press the seam allowances toward the **RED** strip. Make a total of 3 strip sets. Cut the strip sets into segments.

Crosscut 44, 2-1/2-inch wide segments

Step 3
To make the top and bottom checkerboard borders, sew together 9 of the Step 2 segments and press. <u>At this point each strip should measure 4-1/2 x 18-1/2-inches.</u> Sew the checkerboard borders to the quilt and press.

Make 2

QUILTING DESIGNS . . . .

Quilting suggestions for the tree block

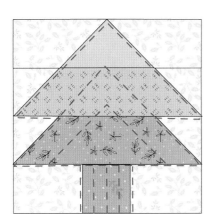

Step 4

To make the side checkerboard borders, sew together 13 of the Step 2 segments and press. <u>At this point each strip should measure 4-1/2 x 26-1/2-inches.</u> Sew the checkerboard borders to the side edges of the quilt and press.

Make 2

PUTTING IT ALL TOGETHER

Trim the backing and batting so they are 4-inches larger than the quilt top. Read through **Finishing the Quilt** on page 118 for complete instructions.

BINDING

Cutting

From **GREEN PRINT #4:**
• Cut 3, 2-3/4 x 42-inch strips

Diagonally piece the strips as needed. Sew the binding to the quilt using a 3/8-inch seam allowance. This measurement will produce a 1/2-inch wide finished double binding. Read through **Binding** instructions on page 119 for complete instructions.

Waiting For Springtime

Yardage is based on 42-inch wide fabric.

Fabrics and Supplies

4-3/4	yards	**PURPLE PRINT** for diamond blocks, inner border, and flying geese border
3-7/8	yards	**GOLD PRINT** for diamond blocks and alternate blocks
3	yards	**BLUE PRINT** for hourglass blocks and corner squares
2-2/3	yards	**BEIGE PRINT** for hourglass blocks
1-2/3	yards	**GREEN PRINT** for flying geese border
1	yard	**GOLD PRINT** for binding
8-5/8	yards	Backing fabric

Quilt batting, at least 100 x 116-inches

A rotary cutter, mat, and wide clear plastic ruler with 1/8-inch markings are needed tools in attaining accuracy. A 6 x 24-inch ruler and 12-1/2-inch acrylic square are recommended.

This beautiful traditional bed quilt is simply made by combining three different blocks and adding a special border that frames the quilt like a picture frame. A simple adjustment from feminine to masculine colors and prints quickly changes this quilt into the perfect "guy" quilt.

96 x 112-inches
Block: 8-inches square

Getting Started

❖ Read instructions thoroughly before beginning project.

❖ Prewash and press fabrics to test for color fastness and possible shrinkage.

❖ For piecing, place right sides of fabric pieces together and use 1/4-inch seam allowances throughout unless otherwise specified.

❖ It is very important that accurate 1/4-inch seam allowances are used. It is wise to stitch a sample 1/4-inch seam allowance to check your machine's seam allowance accuracy.

❖ Press seam allowances in one direction toward the darker fabric and/or in the direction that will create the least bulk.

❖ Instructions are given for quick cutting and piecing of blocks. Note that for some of the pieces, the quick-cutting method will result in leftover fabric.

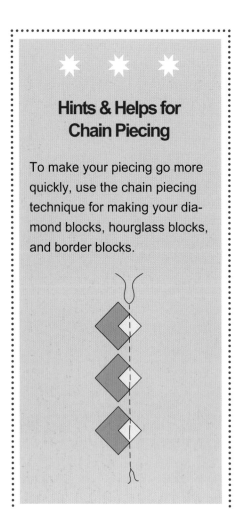

Hints & Helps for Chain Piecing

To make your piecing go more quickly, use the chain piecing technique for making your diamond blocks, hourglass blocks, and border blocks.

"Diamond" Blocks

MAKE 30 BLOCKS

Cutting

From **PURPLE PRINT**:
• Cut 8, 8-1/2 x 42-inch strips. From these strips cut:
    30, 8-1/2-inch squares

From **GOLD PRINT**:
• Cut 14, 4-1/2 x 42-inch strips. From these strips cut:
    120, 4-1/2-inch squares

Piecing

Position a 4-1/2-inch **GOLD** square on the corner of an 8-1/2-inch **PURPLE** square. Draw a diagonal line on the square and stitch on the line. Trim the seam allowance to 1/4-inch and press toward the **GOLD**. Repeat this process for the opposite corner of the **PURPLE** square. Position **GOLD** squares on the remaining 2 corners of the **PURPLE** square, draw a diagonal line on the squares, stitch, trim, and press toward the **GOLD**. <u>At this point each diamond block should measure 8-1/2-inches square.</u>

     Make 30

Hourglass Blocks

MAKE 49 BLOCKS

Cutting

From **BLUE PRINT**:
• Cut 7, 9-1/4 x 42-inch strips. From these strips cut:
    25, 9-1/4-inch squares.   Cut each square twice diagonally to make 100 triangles. You will be using only 98 triangles.

From **BEIGE PRINT**:
• Cut 7, 9-1/4 x 42-inch strips. From these strips cut:
    25, 9-1/4-inch squares. Cut each square twice diagonally to make 100 triangles. You will be using only 98 triangles.

TIP . . . .

- When cutting strips or rectangles, cut on the crosswise grain. Strips can then be cut into squares or smaller rectangles.

- After cutting a few strips, if your strips are not straight, refold the fabric, align the folded and selvage edges with the lines on the cutting board, and "square" off the edge again and begin cutting.

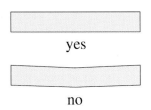

yes

no

TIP . . . .

Stitch on the outer edge just a "hair" or a thread width from the marked diagonal line.

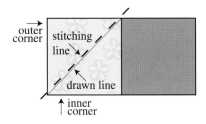

If you stitch on the inner corner side of the diagonal line you will actually make the triangle smaller.

Piecing

Layer a **BLUE** triangle on a **BEIGE** triangle. Stitch along the bias edge as shown, being careful not to stretch as you sew. Press the seam allowance toward the **BLUE** triangle. Repeat for the remaining triangles, stitching along the same bias edge of each triangle set. Sew the triangle units together in pairs and press. <u>At this point each hourglass block should measure 8-1/2-inches square.</u>

Bias edges

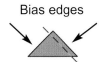

Make 98 triangle units

Make 49 hourglass units

QUILT CENTER

Cutting

From **BLUE PRINT**:
- Cut 6, 4-1/2 x 42-inch strips. From these strips cut:
    22, 4-1/2 x 8-1/2-inch rectangles

From **BEIGE PRINT**:
- Cut 5, 4-1/2 x 42-inch strips. From these strips cut:
    44, 4-1/2-inch squares

From **GOLD PRINT**:
- Cut 5, 8-1/2 x 42-inch strips. From these strips cut:
    20, 8-1/2-inch alternate block squares
- Cut 5, 4-1/2 x 42-inch strips. From these strips cut:
    18, 4-1/2 x 8-1/2-inch rectangles
    4, 4-12-inch squares

Quilt Center Assembly

Step 1

Position a 4-1/2-inch **BEIGE** square on one side of a 4-1/2 x 8-1/2-inch **BLUE** rectangle. Draw a diagonal line on the square, stitch, trim, and press toward light fabric. Repeat this process at the opposite side of the rectangle.

Make 22

Diagonal Piecing

❖ For borders that are longer than 42-inches, piece the border strips together with diagonal seams. They are less visible in a finished quilt than straight seams.

❖ To sew two border strips together diagonally, place them together at a 90° angle with right sides together, as shown below.

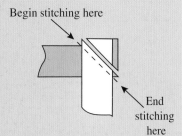

Each strip should extend approximately 1/4-inch beyond the other. Draw a diagonal line to use as your stitching guide. Sew the two strips together, taking care to start and stop your stitching precisely at the point where the two strips meet, as shown above. Trim away the excess fabric, leaving a 1/4-inch seam allowance, and press the seam open.

❖ Cut enough border strips so after your strips are stitched together, the diagonal seams will not be at the corners of the quilt top.

Step 2

To make the top and bottom quilt center strips, sew together 5 of the Step 1 units, 4 of the 4-1/2 x 8-1/2-inch **GOLD** rectangles, and 2 of the 4-1/2-inch **GOLD** squares. Press the seam allowances toward the **GOLD** fabric. At this point each strip should measure 4-1/2 x 80-1/2-inches.

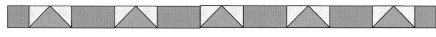

Make 2

Step 3

To make the diamond/hourglass block rows, sew together 5 of the diamond blocks, 4 of the hourglass blocks, and 2 of the Step 1 units. Press the seam allowances toward the diamond blocks. At this point each block row should measure 8-1/2 x 80-1/2-inches.

Make 6

Step 4

To make the hourglass/alternate block rows, sew together 5 of the hourglass blocks, 4 of the 8-1/2-inch **GOLD** alternate blocks, and 2 of the 4-1/2 x 8-1/2-inch **GOLD** rectangles. Press the seam allowances toward the alternate blocks. At this point each block row should measure 8-1/2 x 80-1/2-inches.

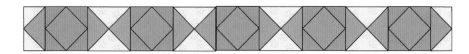

Make 5

Step 5

Referring to the quilt assembly diagram, lay out the strips and block rows from Steps 2, 3, and 4. Pin them together at the block intersections and sew the rows together. Press the row seam allowances in one direction. At this point the quilt center should measure 80-1/2 x 96-1/2-inches.

Quilt Assembly Diagram

QUILTING TIP . . . . .

Because of the simplicity of these quilt blocks, the quilt will be more special if you use a more intricate quilting pattern on the plain alternate blocks and the diamond/hourglass blocks. A great looking way to finish your borders is by "echo" and "channel" quilting. This technique will make the borders stand out.

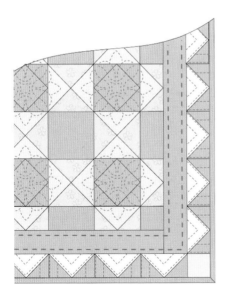

BORDERS

Note: The yardage given allows for the border strips to be cut on the crosswise grain. Diagonally piece the strips as needed. Read through **Borders** on page 118 for general instructions on adding borders.

Cutting

From **PURPLE PRINT**:
- Cut 10, 4-1/2 x 42-inch inner border strips
- Cut 11, 4-1/2 x 42-inch strips. From these strips cut:
      96, 4-1/2-inch squares

From **GREEN PRINT**:
- Cut 12, 4-1/2 x 42-inch strips. From these strips cut:
      48, 4-1/2 x 8-1/2-inch rectangles

From **BLUE PRINT**:
- Cut 4, 4-1/2-inch corner squares

TIP . . . .

In quilts with many "flying geese" units, try this pressing tip: Press the trimmed seams in opposite directions, one seam inward and one seam outward. This will make it easier when stitching several of the units together.

TO MAINTAIN PERFECT FLYING GEESE TIPS ON AN OUTSIDE BORDER . . .

When trimming away the excess batting and backing after quilting, be sure to allow a 3/8-inch seam allowance beyond the points of the "flying geese" tips. By taking a slightly wider seam allowance, you are able to maintain the "points." The extra batting and backing will help fill the binding area.

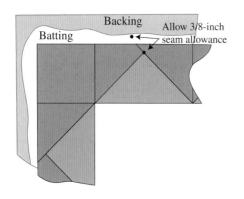

Assembling and Attaching the Borders

Step 1
Attach the 4-1/2-inch wide **PURPLE** inner border strips.

Step 2
Position a 4-1/2-inch **PURPLE** square on one side of a 4-1/2 x 8-1/2-inch **GREEN** rectangle. Draw a diagonal line on the square, stitch, trim, and press toward the **PURPLE**. Repeat the process at the opposite side of the rectangle, but press toward the **GREEN**.

Make 48 flying geese units

Step 3
To make the top and bottom border strips, sew together 11 of the flying geese units and press. At this point each border strip should measure 4-1/2 x 88-1/2-inches. Sew the pieced borders to the quilt center and press toward the **PURPLE** middle border.

Step 4
To make the side border strips, sew together 13 of the flying geese units and press. Sew 4-1/2-inch **BLUE** corner squares to both ends of the border strips and press. At this point each border strip should measure 4-1/2 x 112-1/2-inches. Sew the pieced borders to the quilt center and press towards the **PURPLE** middle border.

PUTTING IT ALL TOGETHER

Cut the 8-5/8 yard length of backing fabric in thirds crosswise to make 3, 2-7/8 yard lengths. Refer to **Finishing the Quilt** on page 118 for complete instructions.

BINDING

Cutting

From **GOLD PRINT:**
• Cut 11, 2-3/4 x 42-inch strips

Sew the binding to the quilt using a 3/8-inch seam allowance. This measurement will produce a 1/2-inch wide finished double binding. Refer to **Binding** and **Diagonal Piecing** instructions on page 119 for complete instructions.

QUILT STENCIL

Trace part or all of this stencil onto various quilts from the Beginner's Luck book.
This stencil is appropriate for hand or machine quilting.

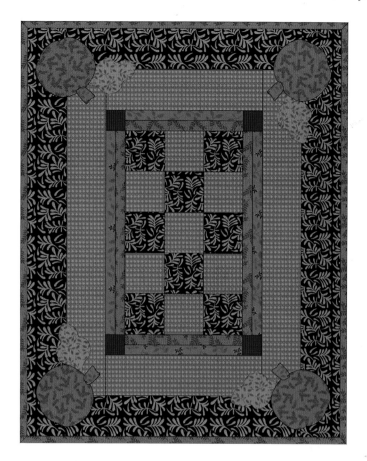

Welcome Home Runner

Yardage is based on 42-inch wide fabric.

Fabrics and Supplies

1/2	yard	**BLACK PRINT #1** for patchwork center and outer border
1/2	yard	**DARK GREEN PRINT** for patchwork center and middle border
1/8	yard	**ORANGE PRINT #1** for first inner border
1/8	yard	**BROWN PRINT** for second inner border and stem appliques
1/8	yard	**BLACK PRINT #2** for corner squares

6 x 42-inch strip **ORANGE PRINT #2** for pumpkin appliques

5 x 20-inch strip **LIGHT GREEN PRINT** for leaf appliques

1/3	yard	**ORANGE PRINT #1** for binding
7/8	yard	Backing fabric
1/2	yard	Freezer paper for appliques

Quilt batting, at least 29 x 35-inches

A rotary cutter, mat, and wide clear plastic ruler with 1/8-inch markings are needed tools in attaining accuracy. A 6 x 24-inch ruler and 12-1/2-inch acrylic square are recommended.

25 x 31-inches

Getting Started

❖ Read instructions thoroughly before beginning project.
❖ Prewash and press fabrics to test for color fastness and possible shrinkage.
❖ For piecing, place right sides of fabric pieces together and use 1/4-inch seam allowances throughout unless otherwise specified.
❖ It is very important that accurate 1/4-inch seam allowances are used. It is wise to stitch a sample 1/4-inch seam allowance to check your machine's seam allowance accuracy.
❖ Press seam allowances in one direction toward the darker fabric and/or in the direction that will create the least bulk.
❖ Instructions are given for quick cutting and piecing of blocks. Note that for some of the pieces, the quick-cutting method will result in leftover fabric.

TIP . . . .

Don't let the applique on this quilt scare you away. Our easy, fool-proof applique technique will carefully guide you through the process and give you the confidence to try other applique quilt patterns.

Use this pattern to make a fun autumn runner--or omit the applique and change the color combinations--and the runner is just right for all seasons.

TIP . . . .

If your patchwork center does not measure 9-1/2 x 15-1/2-inches, make very small adjustments on many seams. The small amounts will be less noticeable than making a large adjustment on one seam.

PATCHWORK CENTER

Cutting

From **BLACK PRINT #1:**
- Cut 1, 3-1/2 x 42-inch strip. From this strip cut:
    8, 3-1/2-inch squares

From **DARK GREEN PRINT:**
- Cut 1, 3-1/2 x 42-inch strip. From this strip cut:
    7, 3-1/2-inch squares

Piecing

Referring to the runner diagram, sew the 3-1/2-inch **BLACK #1** and **DARK GREEN** squares together in 5 rows of 3 squares each. Press each row in opposite directions. Sew the rows together and press. <u>At this point the patchwork center should measure 9-1/2 x 15-1/2-inches.</u>

BORDERS

*Note: The yardage given allows for the border strips to be cut on the crosswise grain. Read through **Border** instructions on page 118 for general instructions on adding borders.*

Cutting

From **ORANGE PRINT #1:**
- Cut 2, 1-1/2 x 42-inch first inner border strips

From **BROWN PRINT:**
- Cut 2, 1-1/2 x 42-inch second inner border strips

From **BLACK PRINT #2:**
- Cut 4, 2-1/2-inch corner squares

From **DARK GREEN PRINT:**
- Cut 3, 3-1/2 x 42-inch middle border strips

From **BLACK PRINT #1:**
- Cut 3, 3-1/2 x 42-inch outer border strips

Attaching the Borders

Step 1

Aligning long edges, sew the 1-1/2 x 42-inch **ORANGE #1** and **BROWN** border strips together and press. Make a total of 2 pieced inner border strips.

Step 2

Measure the runner from left to right through the middle. Measure and mark the border lengths and center points on the pieced inner border strips. Pin the border strips to the runner, stitch, and press. Trim away the excess fabric.

Step 3

For the side borders, measure the runner top including the seam allowances, but not the top and bottom borders. Cut the pieced side borders to this length. Sew a **BLACK #2** corner square to each end of these border strips and press. Sew the borders to the runner and press outward.

Step 4

Attach the 3-1/2-inch wide **DARK GREEN** middle border strips and press outward.

Step 5

Attach the 3-1/2-inch wide **BLACK #1** outer border strips and press outward.

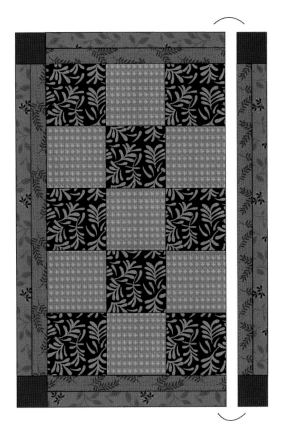

TIP . . . .

For Freezer Paper Applique

It may be easier to applique the shapes if you first hand-baste the pieces onto the quilt top. This will prevent catching the thread on the pins.

Hold the block to be appliqued with your non-sewing hand. Use the side of the needle's point to turn under the seam allowance. Hold the turned-under edge with your thumbnail as you stitch the shape in place.

To make your applique stitches, use a single thread in a matching thread color. Start appliqueing by coming up through the backside of the quilt and catch the edge of the applique shape with your needle. Go back straight down through the quilt and come back up for the next stitch, about 1/16th of an inch away from the previous stitch.

Using size 10 or 11 straw needles gives your applique a great look. They are extra long and flexible and will be easier to guide through the fabric.

QUILTING TIP . . . .

A nice detail for your quilt is to embellish the applique shapes. Add dimension by adding veins to your pumpkins and leaves. Quilting close to these shapes also makes them "pop" out. Channel stitching across the middle and outer borders is a great, quick way to finish off the quilting.

QUILTING DESIGNS . . . .

Quilting suggestions for the Welcome Home Runner

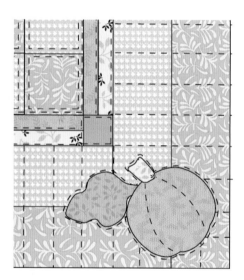

Freezer Paper Applique

With this method of hand-applique, the freezer paper forms a base around which the appliques are shaped.

Step 1 Make templates using the shapes on page 101. Use a pencil to trace the shapes on the non-glossy side of the freezer paper and cut out the shapes on the traced lines.

Step 2 With a hot, dry iron, press the coated side of each freezer paper shape onto the wrong side of the fabric chosen for the appliques. Allow at least 1/2-inch between each shape for seam allowances.

Step 3 Cut out each shape a scant 1/4-inch beyond the edge of the freezer paper pattern. Using a hot, dry iron, press the seam allowance up and over the applique shape. This will not stick to the freezer paper.

Step 4 Referring to the runner diagram for placement, layer and pin the prepared pumpkin, stem, and leaf shapes on the runner top. With your needle, turn the seam allowance over the edge of the freezer paper shape and hand-applique in place. When there is about 3/4-inch left to applique, slide your needle into this opening, loosen the freezer paper from the fabric, and gently pull the freezer paper out. Finish stitching the applique in place.

PUTTING IT ALL TOGETHER

Trim the backing and batting so they are 4-inches larger than the runner top. Refer to **Finishing the Quilt** on page 118 for complete instructions.

BINDING

Cutting

From **ORANGE PRINT #1:**
• Cut 3, 2-3/4 x 42-inch strips

Diagonally piece the strips as needed. Sew the binding to the quilt using a 3/8-inch seam allowance. This measurement will produce a 1/2-inch wide finished double binding. Refer to **Binding** and **Diagonal Piecing** instructions on page 119 for complete instructions.

Welcome Home Runner

The applique shapes are reversed for tracing purposes.
When the applique is finished it will appear as in the diagram.

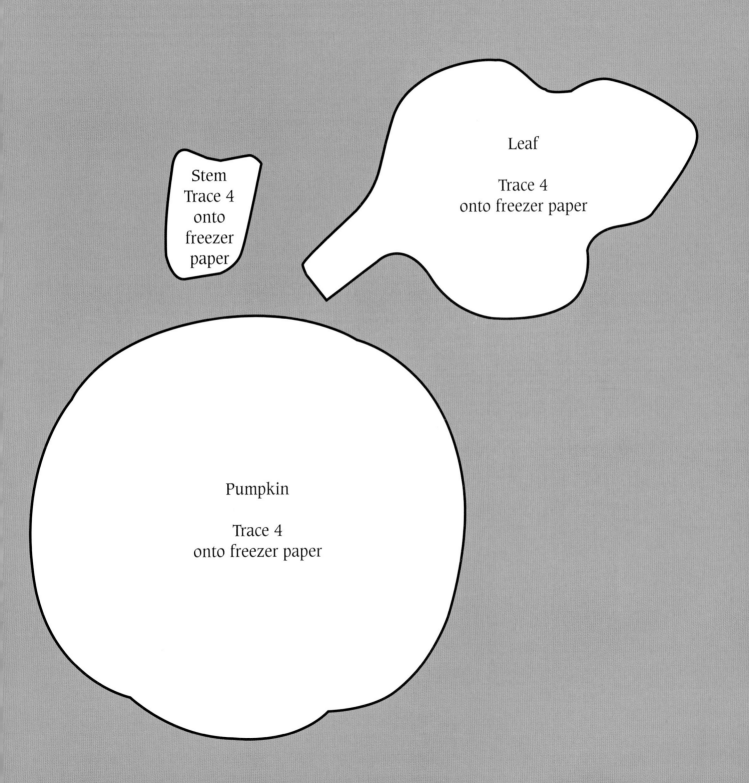

Stem
Trace 4
onto
freezer
paper

Leaf

Trace 4
onto freezer paper

Pumpkin

Trace 4
onto freezer paper

Winter Cottage

Yardage is based on 42-inch wide fabric.

Fabrics and Supplies

1/3	yard	**GREEN PRINT** for tree and grass
7/8	yard	**BEIGE PRINT** for background and checkerboard
3 x 5-inch piece		**BROWN PRINT** for tree trunk
1/4	yard	**GOLD PRINT #1** for star and window
1/2	yard	**BLACK PRINT** for roof, door, and inner border
1	yard	**RED PRINT** for house, checkerboard, and outer border
1/8	yard	**GOLD PRINT #2** for house
3/8	yard	**GOLD PRINT #1** for binding
1-1/4	yards	Backing fabric

Quilt batting, at least 38 x 44-inches

A rotary cutter, mat, and wide clear plastic ruler with 1/8-inch markings are needed tools in attaining accuracy. A 6 x 24-inch ruler and 12-1/2-inch acrylic square are recommended.

A picture perfect quilt made just from squares, rectangles and strips. Sound too simple to be true? Follow the step-by-step instructions and in no time you will have your very own Winter Cottage.

34 x 40-inches

Getting Started

❖ Read instructions thoroughly before beginning project.

❖ Prewash and press fabrics to test for color fastness and possible shrinkage.

❖ For piecing, place right sides of fabric pieces together and use 1/4-inch seam allowances throughout unless otherwise specified.

❖ It is very important that accurate 1/4-inch seam allowances are used. It is wise to stitch a sample 1/4-inch seam allowance to check your machine's seam allowance accuracy.

❖ Press seam allowances in one direction toward the darker fabric and/or in the direction that will create the least bulk.

❖ Instructions are given for quick cutting and piecing of blocks. Note that for some of the pieces, the quick-cutting method will result in leftover fabric.

TIP . . . .

Take extra care when piecing units with corner square triangles. Correct cutting, marking, and stitching can make a big difference on a quilt with many points such as this quilt. Accurate 1/4-inch seam allowances are a must as it will determine how sharp and crisp your points will be.

TIP . . . .

Stitch on the outer edge just a "hair" or a thread width from the marked diagonal line.

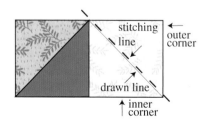

If you stitch on the inner corner side of the diagonal line you will actually make the triangle smaller.

TREE BLOCK

Cutting

From **GREEN PRINT**:
- Cut 1, 4-1/2 x 42-inch strip. From this strip cut:
   1, 4-1/2 x 8-1/2-inch rectangle
   2, 2-1/2 x 8-1/2-inch rectangles
- Cut 1, 2-1/2 x 42-inch strip. From this strip cut:
   4, 2-1/2 x 8-1/2-inch rectangles

From **BEIGE PRINT**:
- Cut 1, 4-1/2 x 42-inch strip. From this strip cut:
   2, 4-1/2-inch squares
   2, 3-1/2 x 4-1/2-inch rectangles
- Cut 1, 2-1/2 x 42-inch strip. From this strip cut:
   12, 2-1/2-inch squares

From **BROWN PRINT**:
- Cut 1, 2-1/2 x 4-1/2-inch rectangle

Piecing

Step 1
Position a 4-1/2-inch **BEIGE** square on the corner of a 4-1/2 x 8-1/2-inch **GREEN** rectangle. Draw a diagonal line on the square and stitch on the line. Trim the seam allowance to 1/4-inch and press. Repeat this process at the opposite corner of the rectangle. <u>At this point the tree top unit should measure 4-1/2 x 8-1/2-inches.</u>

Make 1

Step 2
Position 2-1/2-inch **BEIGE** squares on the corners of a 2-1/2 x 8-1/2-inch **GREEN** rectangle. Draw diagonal lines on the squares, stitch, trim, and press. <u>At this point each unit should measure 2-1/2 x 8-1/2-inches.</u>

Make 6

Step 3

Sew 3-1/2 x 4-1/2-inch **BEIGE** rectangles to both side edges of the 2-1/2 x 4-1/2-inch **BROWN** rectangle and press. At this point the trunk unit should measure 4-1/2 x 8-1/2-inches.

Make 1

Step 4

Referring to the block diagram, sew the Step 1, 2, and 3 units together and press. At this point the tree block should measure 8-1/2 x 20-1/2-inches.

STAR BLOCK

Cutting

From **GOLD PRINT #1**:
- Cut 1, 4-1/2-inch square
- Cut 8, 2-1/2-inch squares

From **BEIGE PRINT**:
- Cut 1, 4-1/2 x 10-1/2-inch rectangle
- Cut 2, 2-1/2 x 42-inch strips. From these strips cut:
    1, 2-1/2 x 10-1/2-inch rectangle
    1, 2-1/2 x 8-1/2-inch rectangle
    4, 2-1/2 x 4-1/2-inch rectangles
    4, 2-1/2-inch squares

Piecing

Step 1

Position a 2-1/2-inch **GOLD #1** square on the corner of a 2-1/2 x 4-1/2-inch **BEIGE** rectangle. Draw a diagonal line on the square, stitch, trim, and press. Repeat this process at the opposite corner of the rectangle.

Make 4

Step 2

Sew Step 1 units to the top and bottom edges of the 4-1/2-inch **GOLD #1** square and press. Sew 2-1/2-inch **BEIGE** squares to both ends of the remaining Step 1 units and press. Sew these units to both side edges of the 4-1/2-inch **GOLD #1** square and press. At this point the star block should measure 8-1/2-inches square.

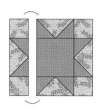

Step 3

Sew the 2-1/2 x 8-1/2-inch **BEIGE** rectangle to the top of the star block and press. Sew the 2-1/2 x 10-1/2-inch **BEIGE** rectangle to the left edge of the star block, and sew the 4-1/2 x 10-1/2-inch **BEIGE** rectangle to the right edge, and press. At this point the star block should measure 10-1/2 x 14-1/2-inches.

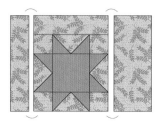

HOUSE BLOCK

Cutting

From **BLACK PRINT:**

- Cut 1, 4-1/2 x 42-inch strip. From this strip cut:
     1, 4-1/2 x 6-1/2-inch rectangle
     1, 4-1/2-inch square
     1, 2-1/2 x 4-1/2-inch rectangle

From **BEIGE PRINT**:

- Cut 2, 4-1/2-inch squares

From **RED PRINT:**

- Cut 1, 4-1/2 x 42-inch strip. From this strip cut:
     1, 4-1/2 x 8-1/2-inch rectangle
     2, 2-1/2 x 6-1/2-inch rectangles
     2, 2-1/2-inch squares

From **GOLD PRINT #1**:

• Cut 1, 2-1/2-inch square

From **GOLD PRINT #2**:

• Cut 1, 3-1/2 x 42-inch strip. From this strip cut:
   2, 3-1/2 x 6-1/2-inch rectangles
   1, 2-1/2-inch square

Piecing

Step 1

Position a 4-1/2-inch **BEIGE** square on the right corner of the 4-1/2 x 6-1/2-inch **BLACK** rectangle. Draw a diagonal line on the square, stitch, trim, and press.

   Make 1

Step 2

Position a 4-1/2-inch **BEIGE** square on the left corner of the 4-1/2 x 8-1/2-inch **RED** rectangle. Draw a diagonal line on the square, stitch, trim, and press. Position a 4-1/2-inch **BLACK** square on the right corner of the rectangle.   Draw a diagonal line on the square, stitch, trim, and press.

     Make 1

Step 3

Sew the Step 1 and Step 2 units together to make the roof unit. <u>At this point the roof unit should measure 4-1/2 x 14-1/2-inches</u>.

Step 4

Sew the 2-1/2-inch **GOLD #2** square to the top edge of the 2-1/2 x 4-1/2-inch **BLACK** rectangle and press. Sew the 3-1/2 x 6-1/2-inch **GOLD #2** rectangles to both side edges of this unit and press.

Step 5

Sew 2-1/2-inch **RED** squares to the top and bottom edges of the 2-1/2-inch **GOLD #1** square and press. Sew the 2-1/2 x 6-1/2-inch **RED** rectangles to both side edges of this unit and press. Sew the Step 4 unit to the left side of this unit and press. <u>At this point the house base unit should measure 6-1/2 x 14-1/2-inches.</u>

Step 6

Sew the Step 3 roof unit to the top of the Step 5 house base unit and press. <u>At this point the house block should measure 10-1/2 x 14-1/2-inches.</u>

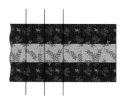

QUILT CENTER

Cutting

From **RED PRINT**:
- Cut 3, 2-1/2 x 18-inch strips

From **BEIGE PRINT**:
- Cut 3, 2-1/2 x 18-inch strips

From **GREEN PRINT**:
- Cut 1, 2-1/2 x 22-1/2-inch strip

Piecing

Step 1

Aligning long edges, sew a 2-1/2 x 18-inch **RED** strip to both sides of a 2-1/2 x 18-inch **BEIGE** strip, and press. Refer to **Hints and Helps for Pressing Strip** sets on page 109. Cut the strip set into segments.

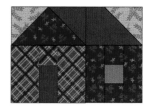

Crosscut 6, 2-1/2-inch
wide segments

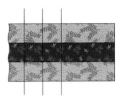

Hints & Helps for Pressing Strip Sets

When sewing strips of fabric together for strip sets, it is important to press the seam allowances nice and flat, usually to the dark fabric. Be careful not to stretch as you press, causing a "rainbow effect." This will affect the accuracy and shape of the pieces cut from the strip set. Press on the wrong side first with the strips perpendicular to the ironing board. Then flip the piece over and press on the right side to prevent little pleats from forming at the seams. Laying the strip set lengthwise on the ironing board seems to encourage the rainbow effect, as shown in diagram.

wrong   right

Step 2

Aligning long edges, sew a 2-1/2 x 18-inch **BEIGE** strip to both sides of a 2-1/2 x 18-inch **RED** strip, and press. Cut the strip set into segments.

Crosscut 5, 2-1/2-inch wide segments

Step 3

Sew the Step 1 and Step 2 segments together to make the checkerboard unit. Sew the 2-1/2 x 22-1/2-inch **GREEN** strip to the top edge of the checkerboard unit and press. At this point the unit should measure 8-1/2 x 22-1/2-inches.

Tip . . . . .

If your checkerboard border does not measure 22-1/2-inches long, make very small adjustments on many seams. The small amounts will be less noticeable than making a large adjustment on one seam.

Make 1

Step 4

Referring to the quilt diagram, sew the tree, star, and house blocks together and press. Sew the Step 3 unit to the bottom edge of this unit and press. At this point the quilt center should measure 22-1/2 x 28-1/2-inches.

Quilt Assembly Diagram

BORDERS

Note: *The yardage given allows for the border strips to be cut on the crosswise grain.* *Read through* **Border** *instructions on page 118 for general instructions on adding borders.*

Cutting

From **BLACK PRINT**:
- Cut 4, 2-1/2 x 42-inch inner border strips

From **RED PRINT**:
- Cut 4, 4-1/2 x 42-inch outer border strips

Attaching the Borders

Step 1
Attach the 2-1/2-inch wide **BLACK** inner border strips.

Step 2
Attach the 4-1/2-inch wide **RED** outer border strips.

Border Assembly Diagram

PUTTING IT ALL TOGETHER

Trim the backing and batting so they are 4-inches larger than the quilt top. Refer to **Finishing the Quilt** on page 118 for complete instructions.

BINDING

Cutting

From **GOLD PRINT #1**:
- Cut 4, 2-3/4 x 42-inch strips

Sew the binding to the quilt using a 3/8-inch seam allowance. This measurement will produce a 1/2-inch wide finished double binding. Refer to **Binding** and **Diagonal Piecing** instructions on page 119 for complete instructions.

Refer to **Finishing the Quilt** on page 118 for complete instructions.

TIP . . . .

To hang wall quilts, try attaching a casing that is made of the same fabric as the quilt back at the top of the quilt. Often, it is helpful to attach a second casing at the bottom of the quilt. That way, you can insert a dowel to help weight the quilt and make it hang free of ripples.

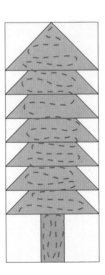

Quilting Diagram option

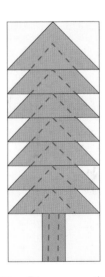

Quilting Diagram option

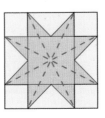

Quilting Diagram

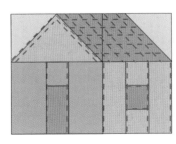

Quilting Diagram

GENERAL INSTRUCTIONS

• Yardage is based on 42-inch wide fabric. If your fabric is wider or narrower it will affect the amount of necessary strips you need to cut in some patterns, and of course, it will affect the amount of fabric you have left over. Generally, THIMBLEBERRIES patterns allow for a little extra fabric so you can confidently cut your pattern pieces with ease.

• A rotary cutter, mat, and wide clear plastic ruler with 1/8-inch markings are needed tools in attaining accuracy. A beginner needs good tools just as an experienced quilt maker needs good equipment. A 24 x 36-inch mat board is a good size to own. It will easily accommodate the average quilt fabrics and will aid in accurate cutting. The plastic ruler you purchase should be at least 6 x 24-inches and easy to read. Do not purchase a smaller ruler to save money, the large size will be invaluable to your quilt making success.

• It is often recommended to prewash and press fabrics to test for color fastness and possible shrinkage. If you choose to prewash, wash in cool water and dry in a cool to moderate dryer. Industry standards actually suggest that line drying is best. Shrinkage is generally very minimal and usually is not a concern. A good way to test your fabric for both shrinkage and color fastness is to cut a 3-inch square of fabric. Soak the fabric in a white bowl filled with water. Squeeze the water out of the fabric and press it dry on a piece of muslin. If the fabric is going to release color it will do so either in the water or when it is pressed dry. Remeasure the 3-inch fabric square to see if it has changed size considerably (more than 1/4-inch). If it has, wash, dry, and press the entire yardage. This little test could save you hours in prewashing and pressing.

• Read instructions thoroughly before beginning a project. Each step will make more sense to you when you have a general overview of the whole process. Take one step at time and follow the illustrations. They will often make more sense to you than the words. Take "baby steps" so you don't get over- whelmed by the entire process.

• When working with flannel and other loosely woven fabrics, always prewash and dry. These fabrics almost always shrink some.

• For piecing, place right sides of the fabric pieces together and use 1/4-inch seam allowances throughout the entire quilt unless otherwise specifically stated in the directions. An accurate seam allowance is the most important part of the quilt making process after accurate cutting. All the directions are based on accurate 1/4-inch seam allowances. It is very important to check your sewing machine to see what position your fabric should be to get accurate seams. To test, use a piece of 1/4-inch graph paper, stitch along the quarter inch line as if the paper where fabric. Make note of where the edge of the paper lines up with your presser foot or where it lines up on the throat plate of your machine. Many quilters place a piece of masking tape on the throat plate to help guide the edge of the fabric. Now test your seam allowance on fabric. Cut 2, 2-1/2-inch squares, place right sides together and stitch along one edge. Press seam allowances in one direction and measure. At this point the unit should measure 2-1/2 x 4-1/2-inches. If it does not, adjust your stitching guidelines and test again. Seam allowances are included in the cutting sizes given in this book.

• Pressing is the third most important step in quilt making. As a general rule, you should never cross a stitched seam with another seam unless it has been pressed. Therefore, every time you stitch a seam it needs to be pressed before adding another piece. Often, it will feel like you press as much as you sew, and often that is true. It is very important that you press and not iron the seams. Pressing is a firm, up and down motion that will flatten the seams but not distort the piecing. Ironing is a back and forth motion and will stretch and distort the small pieces. Most quilters use steam to help the pressing process. The moisture does help and will not distort the shapes as long as the pressing motion is used.

• An old fashioned rule is to press seam allowances in one direction, toward the darker fabric. Often, background fabrics are light in color and pressing toward the darker fabric prevents the seam allowances from showing through to the right side. Pressing seam allowances in one direction is thought to create a stronger seam. Also, for ease in hand-quilting, the quilting lines should fall on the side of the seam which is opposite the seam allowance. As you piece quilts, you will find these "rules" to be helpful but not necessarily always appropriate. Sometimes seams need to be pressed in the opposite direction so the seams of different units will fit together more easily which quilters refer to as seams "nesting" together. When sewing together two units with opposing seam allowances, use the tip of your seam ripper to gently guide the units under your presser foot. Sometimes it is necessary to re-press the seams to make the units fit together nicely. Always try to achieve the least bulk in one spot and accept that no matter which way you press, it may be a little tricky and it could be a little bulky.

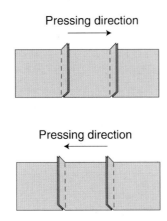

Pressing direction

Pressing direction

Squaring Up Blocks

To square up your blocks, first check the seam allowances. This is usually where the problem is, and it is always best to alter within the block rather than trim the outer edges. Next, make sure you have pressed accurately. Sometimes a block can become distorted by ironing instead of pressing.

To trim up block edges, use one of many clear plastic squares available on the market. Determine the center of the block; mark with a pin. Lay the square over the block and align as many perpendicular and horizontal lines as you can to the seams in your block. This will indicate where the block is off. Do not trim all off on one side; this usually results in real distortion of the pieces in the block and the block design. Take a little off all sides until the block is square. When assembling many blocks, it it necessary to make sure *all* are the same size.

Tools and Equipment

Making beautiful quilts does not require a large number of specialized tools or expensive equipment. My list of favorites is short and sweet, and includes the things I use over and over again because they are always accurate and dependable.

• I find a long acrylic ruler indispensable for accurate rotary cutting. The ones I like most are an Omnigrid 6 x 24-inch grid acrylic ruler for cutting long strips and squaring up fabrics and quilt tops, and a Masterpiece 45, 8 x 24-inch ruler for cutting 6- to 8-inch wide borders. I sometimes tape together two 6 x 24-inch acrylic rulers for cutting borders up to 12-inches wide.

• A 15-inch Omnigrid square acrylic ruler is great for squaring up individual blocks and corners of a quilt top, for cutting strips up to 15-inches wide or long, and for trimming side and corner triangles.

• I think the markings on my 23 x 35-inch Olfa rotary cutting mat stay visible longer than on other mats, and the lines are fine and accurate.

• The largest size Olfa rotary cutter cuts through many layers of fabric easily, and it isn't cumbersome to use. The 2-1/2-inch blade slices through three layers of backing, batting, and a quilt top like butter.

• An 8-inch pair of Gingher shears is great for cutting out applique templates and cutting fabric from a bolt or fabric scraps.

• I keep a pair of 5-1/4-inch Gingher scissors by my sewing machine, so it is handy for both machine work and handwork. This size is versatile and sharp enough to make large and small cuts equally well.

• My Grabbit magnetic pin cushion has a surface that is large enough to hold lots of straight pins, and a strong magnet that keeps them securely in place.

• Silk pins are long and thin, which means they won't leave large holes in your fabric. I like them because they increase accuracy in pinning pieces or blocks together, and it is easy to press over silk pins, as well.

• For pressing individual pieces, blocks, and quilt tops, I use an 18 x 48-inch sheet of plywood covered with several layers of cotton fiberfill and topped with a layer of muslin stapled to the back. The 48-inch length allows me to press an entire width of fabric at one time without the need to reposition it, and the square ends are better than tapered ends on an ironing board for pressing finished quilt tops.

ROTARY CUTTING

• **Safety First!** The blades of a rotary cutter are very sharp and need to be for accurate cutting. Look at a variety of cutters to find one that feels good in your hand. All quality cutters have a safety mechanism to "close" the cutting blade when not in use. After each cut and before laying the rotary cutter down, close the blade. Soon this will become second nature to you and will prevent dangerous accidents. Always keep cutters out of the sight of children. Rotary cutters are very tempting to fiddle with when they are laying around. When your blade is dull or nicked, change it. Damaged blades do not cut accurately and require extra effort that can also result in slipping and injury. Also, always cut away from yourself for safety.

• Fold the fabric in half lengthwise matching the selvage edges.

• "Square off" the ends of your fabric before measuring and cutting pieces. This means that the cut edge of the fabric must be exactly perpendicular to the folded edge which creates a 90° angle. Align the folded and selvage edges of the fabric with the lines on the cutting board, and place a ruled square on the fold. Place a 6 x 24-inch ruler against the side of the square to get a 90° angle. Hold the ruler in place, remove the square, and cut along the edge of the ruler. If you are left-handed, work from the other end of the fabric. Use the lines on your cutting board to help line up fabric, but not to measure and cut strips. Use a ruler for accurate cutting, always checking to make sure your fabric is lined up with horizontal and vertical lines on the ruler.

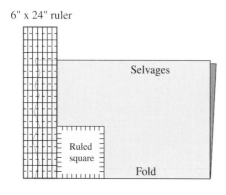

6" x 24" ruler

Cutting Strips

• When cutting strips or rectangles, cut on the cross-wise grain. Strips can then be cut into squares or smaller rectangles.

• If your strips are not straight after cutting a few of them, refold the fabric, align the folded and selvage edges with the lines on the cutting board, and "square off" the edge again by trimming to straighten, and begin cutting.

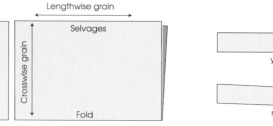
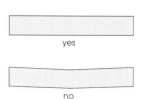

Cutting Side and Corner Triangles

In projects with side and corner triangles, the instructions have you cut side and corner triangles larger than needed. This will allow you to square up the quilt and eliminates the frustration of ending up with precut side and corner triangles that don't match the size of your pieced blocks.

To cut triangles, first cut squares. The project directions will tell you what size to make the squares and whether to cut them in half to make two triangles or to cut them in quarters to make four triangles, as shown in the diagrams. This cutting method will give you side triangles that have the straight of grain on the outside edges of the quilt. This is a very important part of quilt making that will help stabilize your quilt center.

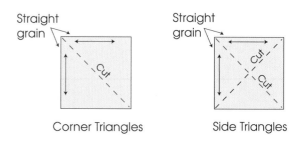

SEWING WITH FLANNEL

- Always prewash and machine dry flannel. This will prevent severe shrinkage after the quilt is made. Some flannels shrink more than others. For this reason, we have allowed approximately 1/4 yard extra for each fabric under the fabric requirements. Treat the more heavily napped side of solid flannels as the right side of the fabric.

- Because flannel stretches more than other cotton calicos and because the nap makes them thicker, the quilt design should be simple. Let the fabric and color make the design statement.

- Consider combining regular cotton calicos with flannels. The different textures complement each other nicely.

- Use a 10 to 12 stitches per inch setting on your machine. A 1/4-inch seam allowance is also recommended for flannel piecing.

- When sewing triangle-pieced squares together, take extra care not to stretch the diagonal seam. Trim off the points from the seam allowances to eliminate bulk.

- Press gently to prevent stretching pieces out of shape.

- Check block measurements as you progress. "Square up" the blocks as needed. Flannel will shift and it is easy to end up with blocks that are misshapen. If you trim and measure as you go, you are more likely to have accurate blocks.

- If you notice a piece of flannel is stretching more than the others, place it on the bottom when stitching on the machine. The natural action of the feed dogs will help prevent it from stretching.

- Before stitching pieces, strips, or borders together, pin often to prevent fabric from stretching and moving. When stitching longer pieces together, divide the pieces into quarters and pin. Divide into even smaller sections to get more control.

- Use a lightweight batting to prevent the quilt from becoming too heavy.

CUTTING TRIANGLES FROM SQUARES

Cutting accurate triangles can be intimidating for beginners, but a clear plastic ruler, rotary cutter, and cutting mat are all that are needed to make perfect triangles. The cutting instructions often direct you to cut strips, then squares, and then triangles.

Sewing Layered Strips Together

When you are instructed to layer strips, right sides together, and sew, you need to take some precautions. Gently lay a strip on top of another carefully lining up the raw edges. Pressing the strips together will hold them together nicely and a few pins here and there will also help. Be careful not to stretch the strips as you sew them together.

Rod Casing or Sleeve to Hang Quilts

Choosing a Quilt Design

To hang wall quilts, attach a casing that is made of the same fabric as the quilt back. Attach this casing at the top of the quilt, just below the binding. Often, it is helpful to attach a second casing at the bottom of the quilt so you can insert a dowel into it which will help weight the quilt and make it hang free of ripples.

To make a rod casing or "sleeve", cut enough strips of fabric equal to the width of the quilt plus 2-inches for side hems. Generally, 6-inch wide strips will accommodate most rods. If you are using a rod with a larger diameter, increase the width of the strips.

Seam the strips together to get the length needed; press. Fold the strip in half lengthwise, wrong sides together. Stitch the long raw edges together with a 1/4-inch seam allowance. Center the seam on the backside of the sleeve; press. The raw edges of the seam will be concealed when the sleeve is stitched to the back of the quilt. Turn under both of the short raw edges; press and stitch to hem the ends. The final measurement should be about 1/2-inch from the quilt edges.

Pin the sleeve to the back of the quilt so the top edge of the sleeve is just below the binding. Hand-stitch the top edge of the sleeve in place, then the bottom edge. Make sure to knot and secure your stitches at each end of the sleeve to make sure it will not pull away from the quilt with use. Slip the rod into the casing. If your wall quilt is not directional, making a sleeve for the bottom edge will allow you to turn your quilt end to end to relieve the stress at the top edge. You could also slip a dowel into the bottom sleeve to help anchor the lower edge of the wall quilt.

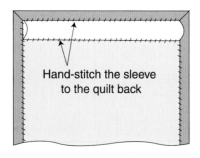

Hand-stitch the sleeve
to the quilt back

Quilting is such an individual process that it is difficult to recommend designs for each quilt. There are hundreds of quilting stencils available at quilt shops. (Templates are used generally for applique shapes; stencils are used for marking quilting designs.)

There are a few suggestion that may help you decide how to quilt your project, depending on how much time you would like to spend quilting. Many quilters now use professional long arm quilting machines or hire someone skilled at running these machines to do the quilting. This, of course, frees up more time to piece.

Quilting Suggestions

•   Repeat one of the design elements in the quilt as part of the quilting design.

•   Two or three parallel rows of echo quilting outside an applique piece will highlight the shape.

•   Stipple or meander quilting behind a feather or central motif will make the primary design more prominent.

•   Look for quilting designs that will cover two or more borders, rather than choosing separate designs for each individual border.

•   Quilting in the ditch of seams is an effective way to get a project quilted without a great deal of time marking the quilt.

Marking the Quilting Design

When marking the quilt top, use a marking tool that will be visible on the quilt fabric and yet will be easy enough to remove. Always test your marking tool on a scrap of fabric before marking the entire quilt.

Along with a multitude of commercial marking tools available, you may find that very thin slivers of hand soap (Dial, Ivory, etc.) work really well for marking medium to dark color fabrics. The thin lines of soap show up nicely and they are easily removed by simply rubbing gently with a piece of like colored fabric.

QUILT BACKING BASICS

Yardage Requirements and Piecing Suggestions

Crib
45 x 60"

2-3/4 yards
Cut 2, 1-3/8 yard lengths

Twin
72 x 90"

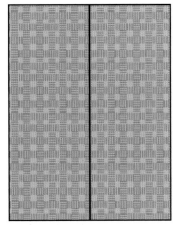

5-1/4 yards
Cut 2, 2-5/8 yard lengths

Double/Full
81 x 96"

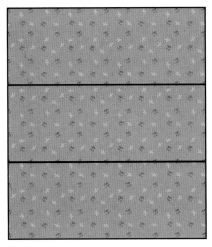

7-1/8 yards
Cut 3, 2-3/8 yard lengths

Queen
90 x 108"

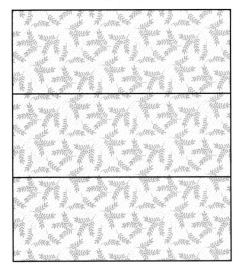

8 yards
Cut 3, 2-5/8 yard lengths

BORDERS

Note . . .

The diagonal seams disguise the piecing better than straight seams. The exception is when a woven plaid is used for a border. It is then best to cut the border strips on the lengthwise grain (parallel to the selvages). When sewing on the bias, sew slowly and do not use too small of a stitch which could cause stretching of the fabric.

Diagonal Piecing

Stitch diagonally

Trim to 1/4" seam allowance

Press seam open

Step 1 With pins, mark the center points along all 4 sides of the quilt. For the top and bottom borders measure the quilt fromm left to right through the middle. This measurement will give you the most accurate measurement that will result in a "square" quilt.

Step 2 Measure and mark the border lengths and center points on the strips cut for the borders before sewing them on.

Step 3 Pin the border strips to the quilt matching the pinned points on each of the borders and the quilt. Pin borders every 6 to 8-inches easing the fabric to fit as necessary. This will prevent the borders and quilt center from stretching while you are sewing them together. Stitch a 1/4-inch seam. Press the seam allowance toward the borders. Trim off excess border lengths.

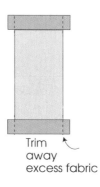
Trim away excess fabric

Step 4 For the side borders, measure your quilt from top to bottom, including the borders just added, to determine the length of the side borders.

Step 5 Measure and mark the side border lengths as you did for the top and bottom borders.

Step 6 Pin and stitch the side border strips in place. When attaching the last two side outer border strips, taking a few backstitches at the beginning and the end of the border will help keep the quilt borders intact during the quilting process. Press and trim the border strips even with the borders just added.

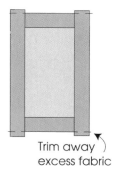
Trim away excess fabric

Step 7 If your quilt has multiple borders, measure, mark, and sew additional borders to the quilt in the same manner.

Finishing the Quilt

Now that your quilt is finished it needs to be layered with batting and backing, and prepared for quilting. Whether it is machine-quilted or hand-quilted, it is best to baste all 3 layers together. You may hand-baste with large basting stitches or pin-baste with medium size brass safety pins. Many quilters are satisfied with spray adhesives which are available at local quilt shops.

Step 1 Press the completed quilt top on the backside first, carefully clipping and removing hanging threads. Then press the quilt front making sure all seams are flat and all loose threads are removed.

Step 2 Remove the selvages from the backing fabric. Sew the long edges together; press. Trim the backing and batting so they are 4-inches larger than the quilt top.

Step 3 Mark the quilt top for quilting. Layer the backing, batting, and quilt top. Baste the 3 layers together and quilt. Work from the center of the quilt out to the edges. This will help keep the quilt flat by working the excess of the 3 layers to the outside edges.

Step 4 When quilting is complete, remove basting. Hand-baste the 3 layers together a scant 1/4-inch from the edge. This basting keeps the layers from shifting and prevents puckers from forming when adding the binding. Trim excess batting and backing fabric even with the edge of the quilt top.

BINDING

The instructions for each quilt indicate the width to cut the binding used in that project. The measurements are sufficient for a quilt made of cotton quilting fabrics and medium low loft quilt batting. If you use a high loft batt or combine a fluffy high loft batt with flannel fabrics, you may want to increase the width of the binding strips by adding 1/4 to 1/2-inch to the cut width of your binding. Always test a small segment of the binding before cutting all the strips needed.

Step 1 Diagonally piece the binding strips. Fold the strip in half lengthwise, wrong sides together; press.

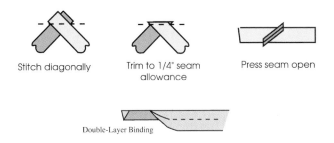

Stitch diagonally   Trim to 1/4" seam allowance   Press seam open

Double-Layer Binding

Step 2 Unfold and trim one end at a 45° angle. Turn under the edge 1/4-inch; press. Refold the strip.

Fold Line

Step 3 With raw edges of the binding and quilt top even, stitch with a 3/8-inch seam allowance, unless otherwise specified, starting 2-inches from the angled end.

Step 4 Miter the binding at the corners. As you approach a corner of the quilt, stop sewing 3/8 to 1-inch from the corner of the quilt (use the same measurement as your seam allowance). Generally, a 3/8-inch seam allowance is used for regular cotton quilts and often a 1-inch seam allowance is used for flannel quilts. Each project in this book gives specific instructions for the binding width and seam allowance to be used.

3/8" to 1"
Binding Strip
Quilt Top

Step 5 Clip the threads and remove the quilt from under the presser foot.

Step 6 Flip the binding strip up and away from the quilt, then fold the binding down even with the raw edge of the quilt. Begin sewing at the upper edge. Miter all 4 corners in this manner.

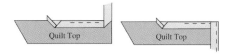

Quilt Top   Quilt Top

Step 7 Trim the end of the binding so it can be tucked inside of the beginning binding about 1/2-inch. Finish stitching the seam.

Quilt Top   Quilt Top

Step 8 Turn the folded edge of the binding over the raw edges and to the back of the quilt so that the stitching line does not show. The corners will naturally turn with very little effort. Pin as needed to create a nice mitered corner on the back as well as on the front. Slip stitch the binding to the backside of the quilt by hand. To do this, slip your needle into the quilt back, sliding the needle approximately 1/4-inch. Bring it out of the fabric again and catch a few threads in the fold of the binding. At exactly the same point from which the needle emerged, insert it into the quilt back again, and take the next stitch. It is a good idea to take a double stitch approximately every 6 to 8-inches to anchor the binding.

Quilt Back   Quilt Back   Quilt Back

SUGGESTED PUBLICATIONS FOR BEGINNER QUILTERS

The Thimbleberries Book of Quilts, Rodale Press

At Home with Thimbleberries Quilts, Rodale Press

The Thimbleberries Guide for Weekend Quilters, Rodale Press

The Quilter's Ultimate Visual Guide, Rodale Press

A Thimbleberries Housewarming, C&T Publishing

Cozy Cabin Quilts from Thimbleberries, C&T Publishing

Town & Country Flannel Quilts, A Thimbleberries Publication

Fireside Flannel Quilts, A Thimbleberries Publication

To complement our line of patterns and books, look for **Thimbleberries** fabrics distributed by RJR Fashion Fabrics and found in quality quilt shops. **Thimbleberries, Inc**. offers a complete line of patterns and books for quilts and creative accessories. For more information visit our web site at www.thimbleberries.com or write for a catalog to:

Thimbleberries
7 North Main Street
Hutchinson, MN 55350